Leslie County, Kentucky Marriages

1884–1894

Richard E. Sampson **and**
Margaret B. Sampson

HERITAGE BOOKS
2010

HERITAGE BOOKS
AN IMPRINT OF HERITAGE BOOKS, INC.

Books, CDs, and more—Worldwide

For our listing of thousands of titles see our website at
www.HeritageBooks.com

Published 2010 by
HERITAGE BOOKS, INC.
Publishing Division
100 Railroad Ave. #104
Westminster, Maryland 21157

Copyright © 1999
Richard E. Sampson and Margaret B. Sampson

Other books by the authors:
Descendants of Thomas Begley
Leslie County, Kentucky, Marriages, 1894–1909
CD: The Lewis Family of Appalachia

All rights reserved. No part of this book may be reproduced or transmitted in any form or by any means, electronic or mechanical, including photocopying, recording or by any information storage and retrieval system without written permission from the author, except for the inclusion of brief quotations in a review.

International Standard Book Numbers
Paperbound: 978-0-7884-1380-3
Clothbound: 978-0-7884-8518-3

Introduction

Leslie County is located in Eastern Kentucky. It has an area of approximately 412 square miles. The county seat is Hyden. Leslie County was established on March 29, 1878 with an effective date of April 15, 1878. It was named after Preston Hopkins Leslie the twenty-sixth governor of Kentucky. Leslie County was formed from three counties, Perry County, Clay County, and Harlan County and the boundaries have remained unchanged.

The county is located on the Middle Fork of the Kentucky River which runs through the middle of the county. The county is full of coal, oil and natural gas. Some iron is also found in the county. The county is also rich in timber.

The early 1800's saw the settlers start to arrive in the area that would eventually become Leslie County. They came from Virginia, North Carolina and Tennessee. They traveled in family groups through the Cumberland Gap or in many cases across the mountains. Quite often more than one family traveled together to arrive at the fertile and well watered valleys of the area. Upon arriving they saw a forested land covered with hardwoods such as oak and maples interlaced with pine.

The early marriage books of Leslie County are in bound volumes on large paper pages. All the books were microfilmed in 1988 by the Kentucky Department of Archives and Libraries. This was prepared from one of the microfilms.

The early marriage books that were in being at the time of the microfilming were as follows:

Marriage Book 1	1878-1885
Marriage Book 2 (Colored)	1878-1913
Marriage Book 3	Did not exist in 1988
Marriage Book 4	Did not exist in 1988
Marriage Book 5	Did not exist in 1988
Marriage Book 6	Did not exist in 1988
Marriage Book 7	1884-1895
Marriage Book 7A	1895-1905

Some time after the microfilming was accomplished, the books were rebound and renumbered in the Leslie County Clerk's Office. The numbers with the exception of Marriage Book 1 do not agree with the current book number in the County Clerk's Office.

Throughout the book there are references to notes. The notes were loose slips of paper placed in the book by the clerk generally showing that permission was given for an underage child to marry. In some cases more that one note was found with a page and the notes in the remarks are separated by "//". In some cases the note apparently fell out of the book and was placed with another page and in these cases the dates or the names do not match up with the marriage shown on the page. The notes were placed in the remarks of the page on which they were found.

Marriages

Abshier

Groom: J. A. Abshier Residence: Leslie County, Kentucky Age: 50 Number of Marriages: 1 Occupation: Shoemaker Groom's POB: Virginia Groom's father POB: Virginia Groom's mother POB: Virginia
Date of marriage: 14 November 1891
Bride: Margaret Lewis Residence: Leslie County, Kentucky Age: 21 Number of Marriages: 1 Bride's POB: Perry County, Kentucky Bride's father POB: Harlan County, Kentucky Bride's mother POB: Harlan County, Kentucky Marriage Book 7, page 453

Adams

Groom: John Adams Residence: Perry County, Kentucky Age: 28 Number of Marriages: Blank Occupation: Farmer and logger Groom's POB: Perry County, Kentucky Groom's father POB: Letcher County, Kentucky Groom's mother POB: Letcher County, Kentucky
Date of marriage: 27 March 1894
Bride: Martha Baker Residence: Leslie County, Kentucky Age: 18 Number of Marriages: Blank Bride's POB: Perry County, Kentucky Bride's father POB: Blank Bride's mother POB: Blank
Remarks: The following note appears in the record: "March 24, 1894. The Clerk of Leslie County. Hereby command to give Martha Baker her license. This is from. Signed: Henry Baker Signed: Cathy Baker."
Marriage Book 7, page 593

Anderson

Groom: Christopher Anderson Residence: Leslie County, Kentucky Age: 18 Number of Marriages: Blank Occupation: Farmer Groom's POB: Perry County, Kentucky Groom's father POB: Tennessee Groom's mother POB: Perry County, Kentucky
Date of marriage: 7 January 1891
Bride: Manda Jane Wooton Residence: Leslie County, Kentucky Age: 19 Number of Marriages: Blank Bride's POB: Perry County, Kentucky Bride's father POB: Perry County, Kentucky Bride's mother POB: Perry County, Kentucky
Remarks: The following note appears in the record: "September 23rd, 1890. I hereby acknowledge that Tabitha Ellen Collins is 21 years old and is given

up to Ulysses G. Collins. Given under my hand. Signed: His mark "X" Robert Collins."
Marriage Book 7, page 409

Asher

Groom: Andrew Asher Residence: Leslie County, Kentucky Age: 24 Number of Marriages: Blank Occupation: Farmer Groom's POB: Perry County, Kentucky Groom's father POB: Blank Groom's mother POB: Blank
Date of marriage: 21 April 1890
Bride: Martha Roberts Residence: Leslie County, Kentucky Age: 25 Number of Marriages: Blank Bride's POB: Perry County, Kentucky Bride's father POB: Blank Bride's mother POB: Blank Marriage Book 7, page 367

Groom: John Asher Residence: Leslie County, Kentucky Age: 20 Number of Marriages: Blank Occupation: Farmer Groom's POB: Perry County, Kentucky Groom's father POB: Blank Groom's mother POB: Blank
Date of marriage: 1 April 1886
Bride: Rachel Jane Feltner Residence: Leslie County, Kentucky Age: Blank Number of Marriages: Blank Bride's POB: Perry County, Kentucky Bride's father POB: Blank Bride's mother POB: Blank Marriage Book 7, page 63

Groom: John Asher Residence: Leslie County, Kentucky Age: 42 Number of Marriages: 2 Occupation: Farmer Groom's POB: Clay County, Kentucky Groom's father POB: Clay County, Kentucky Groom's mother POB: Harlan County, Kentucky
Date of marriage: 4 October 1892
Bride: Emily Lewis Residence: Leslie County, Kentucky Age: 22 Number of Marriages: 1 Bride's POB: Blank Bride's father POB: Blank Bride's mother POB: Blank Marriage Book 7, page 509

Groom: Randall Asher Residence: Leslie County, Kentucky Age: 20 Number of Marriages: 1 Occupation: Farmer Groom's POB: Clay County, Kentucky Groom's father POB: Clay County, Kentucky Groom's mother POB: Clay County, Kentucky
Date of marriage: 14 December 1887
Bride: Mahala Shepherd Residence: Leslie County, Kentucky Age: 19 Number of Marriages: 1 Bride's POB: Perry County, Kentucky Bride's father POB: Perry County, Kentucky Bride's mother POB: Perry County, Kentucky Marriage Book 7, page 181

Groom: Timothy Asher Residence: Leslie County, Kentucky Age: 26
Number of Marriages: Blank Occupation: Farmer Groom's POB: Clay
County, Kentucky Groom's father POB: Clay County, Kentucky Groom's
mother POB: Clay County, Kentucky
Date of marriage: 3 August 1889
Bride: Susannah Ledford Residence: Leslie County, Kentucky Age: 16
Number of Marriages: Blank Bride's POB: Clay County, Kentucky Bride's
father POB: Clay County, Kentucky Bride's mother POB: Clay County,
Kentucky
Remarks: Note appears in the record as follows: "Mr. Clerk. Sir, Let
Timothy Asher have his license to marry my daughter, Susannah Ledford.
This August 2nd, 1889. Signed Granville Ledford Attest: James Clark."
Marriage Book 7, page 301

Ausburn

Groom: Levi Ausburn Residence: Leslie County, Kentucky Age: 18
Number of Marriages: Blank Occupation: Farmer Groom's POB: Clay
County, Kentucky Groom's father POB: Clay County, Kentucky Groom's
mother POB: Clay County, Kentucky
Date of marriage: 8 October 1888
Bride: Louisa Freeman Residence: Leslie County, Kentucky Age: 21
Number of Marriages: Blank Bride's POB: Clay County, Kentucky Bride's
father POB: Blank Bride's mother POB: Blank Marriage Book 7, page 245

Groom: Levi Ausburn Residence: Leslie County, Kentucky Age: 23
Number of Marriages: 1 Occupation: Farmer Groom's POB: Clay County,
Kentucky Groom's father POB: Clay County, Kentucky Groom's mother
POB: Clay County, Kentucky
Date of marriage: 21 November 1892
Bride: Cordelia Jones Residence: Leslie County, Kentucky Age: 22 Number
of Marriages: 1 Bride's POB: Perry County, Kentucky Bride's father POB:
Perry County, Kentucky Bride's mother POB: Perry County, Kentucky
Marriage Book 7, page 521

Bailey

Groom: J. M. Bailey Residence: Hyden, Leslie County, Kentucky Age: 27
Number of Marriages: Blank Occupation: Farmer Groom's POB: Harlan
County, Kentucky Groom's father POB: Virginia Groom's mother POB:
Kentucky
Date of marriage: 9 November 1884
Bride: Mallie French Residence: Harlan County, Kentucky Age: 21
Number of Marriages: Blank Bride's POB: Harlan County, Kentucky

Bride's father POB: Virginia Bride's mother POB: Harlan County, Kentucky Marriage Book 7, page 5

Groom: Minter Bailey Residence: Wooton's Creek, Kentucky Age: 40 Number of Marriages: 1 Occupation: Farmer Groom's POB: Perry County, Kentucky Groom's father POB: Perry County, Kentucky Groom's mother POB: Perry County, Kentucky
Date of marriage: 18 April 1890
Bride: Louisa Baker Residence: Wooton's Creek, Kentucky Age: 30 Number of Marriages: 2 Bride's POB: Perry County, Kentucky Bride's father POB: Perry County, Kentucky Bride's mother POB: Perry County, Kentucky Marriage Book 7, page 365

Baker

Groom: Adam Baker Residence: Wooton Creek, Kentucky Age: 18 Number of Marriages: Blank Occupation: Farmer Groom's POB: Perry County, Kentucky Groom's father POB: Perry County, Kentucky Groom's mother POB: Perry County, Kentucky
Date of marriage: 17 February 1892
Bride: Nannie Wooton Residence: Wooton Creek, Kentucky Age: 18 Number of Marriages: Blank Bride's POB: Perry County, Kentucky Bride's father POB: Perry County, Kentucky Bride's mother POB: Perry County, Kentucky
Remarks: The following note appears in the record: "Mr. J. M. Howard. You are authorized to issue marriage license to Adam Baker, This February 17, 1892. Signed: Russel Baker."
Marriage Book 7, page 483

Groom: Samuel Baker Residence: Leslie County, Kentucky Age: 21 Number of Marriages: 1 Occupation: Farmer Groom's POB: Virginia Groom's father POB: Virginia Groom's mother POB: Virginia
Date of marriage: 19 November 1887
Bride: Phoebe Pennington Residence: Leslie County, Kentucky Age: 18 Number of Marriages: 1 Bride's POB: Perry County, Kentucky Bride's father POB: Perry County, Kentucky Bride's mother POB: Perry County, Kentucky Marriage Book 7, Page 179

Groom: William Baker Residence: Leslie County, Kentucky Age: 35 Number of Marriages: 2 Occupation: Farmer Groom's POB: Perry County, Kentucky Groom's father POB: Perry County, Kentucky Groom's mother POB: Letcher County, Kentucky
Date of marriage: 30 September 1887

Bride: El Jane Baker Residence: Leslie County, Kentucky Age: 21 Number of Marriages: Blank Bride's POB: Perry County, Kentucky Bride's father POB: Perry County, Kentucky Bride's mother POB: Perry County, Kentucky Marriage Book 7, page 169

Barger

Groom: Delaney Barger Residence: Leslie County, Kentucky Age: 51 Number of Marriages: 1 Occupation: Farmer Groom's POB: Clay County, Kentucky Groom's father POB: Clay County, Kentucky Groom's mother POB: Blank
Date of marriage: 4 December 1889
Bride: Jan Browning Residence: Leslie County, Kentucky Age: 26 Number of Marriages: 1 Bride's POB: Perry County, Kentucky Bride's father POB: Harlan County, Kentucky Bride's mother POB: Harlan County, Kentucky Marriage Book 7, page 345

Begley

Groom: Abner Begley Residence: Leslie County, Kentucky Age: 22 Number of Marriages: Blank Occupation: Farmer Groom's POB: Perry County, Kentucky Groom's father POB: Blank Groom's mother POB: Blank
Date of marriage: 27 June 1894
Bride: Elizabeth Hignight Residence: Leslie County, Kentucky Age: 26 Number of Marriages: 1 Bride's POB: Blank Bride's father POB: Blank Bride's mother POB: Blank Marriage Book 7, page 613

Groom: Elijah Begley Residence: Perry County, Kentucky Age: 22 Number of Marriages: Blank Occupation: Farmer Groom's POB: Perry County, Kentucky Groom's father POB: Clay County, Kentucky Groom's mother POB: Clay County, Kentucky
Date of marriage: 25 November 1889
Bride: Sarah Smith Residence: Perry County, Kentucky Age: 21 Number of Marriages: Blank Bride's POB: Perry County, Kentucky Bride's father POB: Harlan County, Kentucky Bride's mother POB: Perry County, Kentucky Marriage Book 7, page 339

Groom: F. G. Begley Residence: Leslie County, Kentucky Age: 23 Number of Marriages: Blank Occupation: School teacher Groom's POB: Clay County, Kentucky Groom's father POB: Blank Groom's mother POB: Blank
Date of marriage: 19 August 1892

Bride: Margaret Boggs Residence: Leslie County, Kentucky Age: 17 Number of Marriages: Blank Bride's POB: Perry County, Kentucky Bride's father POB: Letcher County, Kentucky Bride's mother POB: Blank Remarks: The following note appears in the record: "On the stationary of J. C. Boggs, dealer in General Merchandise, Hazard, Kentucky. August 19, 1892. This is to certify that I have given my consent for the marriage of Felix G. Begley and Margaret Boggs and authorize J. M. Howard or deputy to issue a marriage license for same. Signed: J. C. Boggs."
Marriage Book 7, page 505

Groom: Garret Begley Residence: Perry County, Kentucky Age: 25 Number of Marriages: Blank Occupation: Farmer Groom's POB: Perry County, Kentucky Groom's father POB: Clay County, Kentucky Groom's mother POB: Clay County, Kentucky
Date of marriage: 25 November 1889
Bride: Parilee Baker Residence: Leslie County, Kentucky Age: 21 Number of Marriages: Blank Bride's POB: Perry County, Kentucky Bride's father POB: Blank Bride's mother POB: Blank Marriage Book 7, page 337

Groom: Granville Begley Residence: Leslie County, Kentucky Age: 35 Number of Marriages: 1 Occupation: Farmer Groom's POB: Perry County, Kentucky Groom's father POB: Perry County, Kentucky Groom's mother POB: Perry County, Kentucky
Date of marriage: 24 December 1892
Bride: Chaney Sizemore Residence: Leslie County, Kentucky Age: 25 Number of Marriages: Blank Bride's POB: Clay County, Kentucky Bride's father POB: Blank Bride's mother POB: Blank Marriage Book 7, page 531

Groom: John Y. Begley Residence: Leslie County, Kentucky Age: 52 Number of Marriages: 1 Occupation: Farmer Groom's POB: Perry County, Kentucky Groom's father POB: Perry County, Kentucky Groom's mother POB: Tennessee
Date of marriage: 6 November 1890
Bride: Ellen Hignight Residence: Leslie County, Kentucky Age: 17 Number of Marriages: Blank Bride's POB: Perry County, Kentucky Bride's father POB: Knox County, Kentucky Bride's mother POB: Perry County, Kentucky Marriage Book 7, page 403

Groom: Lafayette Begley Residence: Leslie County, Kentucky Age: 21 Number of Marriages: Blank Occupation: Farmer Groom's POB: Perry County, Kentucky Groom's father POB: Perry County, Kentucky Groom's mother POB: Perry County, Kentucky
Date of marriage: 22 September 1890

Bride: Lucy Ann Baker Residence: Leslie County, Kentucky Age: 16 Number of Marriages: Blank Bride's POB: Perry County, Kentucky Bride's father POB: Perry County, Kentucky Bride's mother POB: Perry County, Kentucky Marriage Book 7, page 395

Groom: Robert Begley Residence: Leslie County, Kentucky Age: 21 Number of Marriages: 1 Occupation: Farmer Groom's POB: Perry County, Kentucky Groom's father POB: Perry County, Kentucky Groom's mother POB: Perry County, Kentucky
Date of marriage: 12 August 1892
Bride: Elizabeth Begley Residence: Leslie County, Kentucky Age: 21 Number of Marriages: 2 Bride's POB: Blank Bride's father POB: Blank Bride's mother POB: Blank Marriage Book 7, page 501

Bentley

Groom: W. P. Bentley Residence: Hyden, Kentucky Age: 28 Number of Marriages: Blank Occupation: Attorney at Law Groom's POB: Blank Groom's father POB: Blank Groom's mother POB: Blank
Date of marriage: 27 April 1888
Bride: Nancy Melton Residence: Hyden, Kentucky Age: 26 Number of Marriages: Blank Bride's POB: Perry County, Kentucky Bride's father POB: Clay County, Kentucky Bride's mother POB: Letcher County, Kentucky Marriage Book 7, page 225

Boggs

Groom: Timothy Boggs Residence: Leslie County, Kentucky Age: 22 Number of Marriages: Blank Occupation: Farmer Groom's POB: Perry County, Kentucky Groom's father POB: Virginia Groom's mother POB: Perry County, Kentucky
Date of marriage: 21 February 1887
Bride: Sarah Coots Residence: Leslie County, Kentucky Age: 18 Number of Marriages: Blank Bride's POB: Perry County, Kentucky Bride's father POB: Perry County, Kentucky Bride's mother POB: Perry County, Kentucky Marriage Book 7, page 127

Bollin

Groom: Pallis Bolin Residence: Leslie County, Kentucky Age: 65 Number of Marriages: 1 Occupation: Farmer Groom's POB: Clay County, Kentucky Groom's father POB: Blank Groom's mother POB: Blank
Date of marriage: 17 May 1889

Bride: Mary Hampton Residence: Leslie County, Kentucky Age: 40 Number of Marriages: 1 Bride's POB: Blank Bride's father POB: Blank Bride's mother POB: Blank Marriage Book 7, page 295

Bowling

Groom: William Bowling Residence: Clay County, Kentucky Age: 23 Number of Marriages: 1 Occupation: Farmer Groom's POB: Clay County, Kentucky Groom's father POB: Clay County, Kentucky Groom's mother POB: Clay County, Kentucky
Date of marriage: 9 February 1888
Bride: Merica Clarkston Residence: Leslie County, Kentucky Age: 22 Number of Marriages: 1 Bride's POB: Clay County, Kentucky Bride's father POB: Lee County, Virginia Bride's mother POB: Clay County, Kentucky Marriage Book 7, page 199

Bond

Groom: Preston Bond Residence: Leslie County, Kentucky Age: 28 Number of Marriages: Blank Occupation: Lawyer Groom's POB: Anderson County, Kentucky Groom's father POB: Anderson County, Kentucky Groom's mother POB: Knox County, Kentucky
Date of marriage: 8 March 1886
Bride: Mary Jane South Residence: Leslie County, Kentucky Age: 18 Number of Marriages: Blank Bride's POB: Clay County, Kentucky Bride's father POB: Blank Bride's mother POB: Blank Marriage Book 7, Page 51

Brock

Groom: Washington Brock Residence: Leslie County, Kentucky Age: 30 Number of Marriages: 1 Occupation: Farmer Groom's POB: Blank Groom's father POB: Blank Groom's mother POB: Blank
Date of marriage: 25 September 1886
Bride: Elizabeth Napier Residence: Leslie County, Kentucky Age: 30 Number of Marriages: 1 Bride's POB: Blank Bride's father POB: Blank Bride's mother POB: Blank Marriage Book 7, Page 105

Brown

Groom: J. C. Brown Residence: Blank Age: Blank Number of Marriages: Blank Occupation: Blank Groom's POB: Blank Groom's father POB: Blank Groom's mother POB: Blank
Date of marriage: 10 December 1891

Bride: Nancy Brock Residence: Blank Age: Blank Number of Marriages: Blank Bride's POB: Blank Bride's father POB: Blank Bride's mother POB: Blank
Remarks: Marriage bond was completed along with marriage certificate.
Marriage Book 7, page 473

Browning

Groom: Don Juan Browning Residence: Leslie County, Kentucky Age: 21 Number of Marriages: 1 Occupation: Farmer Groom's POB: Perry County, Kentucky Groom's father POB: Harlan County, Kentucky Groom's mother POB: Harlan County, Kentucky
Date of marriage: 16 February 1888
Bride: Julyan Howard Residence: Leslie County, Kentucky Age: 16 Number of Marriages: 1 Bride's POB: Leslie County, Kentucky (This is an error, as Leslie County was not formed until 1878. Bride's father POB: Harlan County, Kentucky Bride's mother POB: Perry County, Kentucky
Marriage Book 7, page 203

Burns

Groom: Abijah Burns Residence: Clay County, Kentucky Age: 18 Number of Marriages: Blank Occupation: Farmer Groom's POB: Clay County, Kentucky Groom's father POB: Blank Groom's mother POB: Blank
Date of marriage: 13 March 1889
Bride: Armildia Hoskins Residence: Leslie County, Kentucky Age: 22 Number of Marriages: Blank Bride's POB: Clay County, Kentucky Brides father POB: Clay County, Kentucky Bride's mother POB: Clay County, Kentucky
Remarks: Note appears in the record as follows: "Mr. J. M. Howard, Clerk of Leslie County Court. You are hereby authorized to give license for my son, Abijah Burns and Armildia Hoskins to marry. This 13th Day of March 1889. Signed William Osbourne."
Marriage Book 7, page 279

Caldwell

Groom: J. M. Caldwell Residence: Leslie County, Kentucky Age: 27 Number of Marriages: 1 Occupation: Farmer Groom's POB: Harlan County, Kentucky Groom's father POB: Harlan County, Kentucky Groom's mother: POB: Harlan County, Kentucky
Date of marriage: 5 August 1885
Bride: Francis Blevins Residence: Leslie County, Kentucky Age: Blank Number of Marriages: Blank Bride's POB: Leslie County, Kentucky (This

is an error, as Leslie County did not exist until 1878.) Bride's father POB: Blackwater, Tennessee Bride's mother POB: Harlan County, Kentucky
Marriage Book 7, page 13

Campbell

Groom: Abijah Campbell Residence: Jackson County, Kentucky Age: 22 Number of Marriages: Blank Occupation: Farmer Groom's POB: Perry County, Kentucky Groom's father POB: Blank Groom's mother POB: Blank
Date of marriage: 9 January 1892
Bride: Hannah Bailey Residence: Leslie County, Kentucky Age: 22 Number of Marriages: Blank Bride's POB: Perry County, Kentucky Bride's father POB: Blank Bride's mother POB: Blank Marriage Book 7, page 469

Groom: William Campbell Residence: Perry County, Kentucky Age: 21 Number of Marriages: Blank Occupation: Farmer Groom's POB: Perry County, Kentucky Groom's father POB: Perry County, Kentucky Groom's mother POB: Perry County, Kentucky
Date of marriage: 15 March 1885
Bride: Ellen Sisemore Residence: Leslie County, Kentucky Age: 19 Number of Marriages: Blank Bride's POB: Clay County, Kentucky Bride's father POB: Clay County, Kentucky Bride's mother POB: Breathitt County, Kentucky Marriage Book 7, Page 7

Collett

Groom: James Collett Residence: Leslie County, Kentucky Age: 21 Number of Marriages: Blank Occupation: Farmer Groom's POB: Bell County, Kentucky Groom's father POB: Bell County, Kentucky Groom's mother POB: Bell County, Kentucky
Date of marriage: 5 August 1886
Bride: Siseme Shepherd Residence: Leslie County, Kentucky Age: 16 Number of Marriages: Blank Bride's POB: Clay County, Kentucky Bride's father POB: Blank Bride's mother POB: Blank
Remarks: Note in the record reads as follows: "August 4. You can give James Collett license to marry my daughter Siseme Shepherd. Signed by Tilda Shepherd. Sent by Jackson Collett."
Marriage Book 7, page 89

Groom: W. J. Collett Residence: Leslie County, Kentucky Age: 42 Number of Marriages: 2 Occupation: Farmer Groom's POB: Clay County, Kentucky Groom's father POB: Clay County, Kentucky Groom's mother POB: Blank

Date of marriage: 25 September 1886
Bride: Nancy Collett Residence: Leslie County, Kentucky Age: 17
Number of Marriages: Blank Bride's POB: Clay County, Kentucky Bride's father POB: Clay County, Kentucky Bride's mother POB: Blank Marriage Book 7, page 107

Collins

Groom: George Collins Residence: Leslie County, Kentucky Age: 22
Number of Marriages: 1 Occupation: Farmer Groom's POB: Perry County, Kentucky Groom's father POB: Perry County, Kentucky Groom's mother POB: Perry County, Kentucky
Date of marriage: 6 June 1893
Bride: Merica Barger Residence: Leslie County, Kentucky Age: 18 Number of Marriages: 1 Bride's POB: Perry County, Kentucky Bride's father POB: Perry County, Kentucky Bride's mother POB: Perry County, Kentucky Marriage Book 7, page 551

Groom: Henry Collins Residence: Leslie County, Kentucky Age: 24
Number of Marriages: Blank Occupation: Farmer Groom's POB: Clay County, Kentucky Groom's father POB: Tennessee Groom's mother POB: Clay County, Kentucky
Date of marriage: 14 July 1894
Bride: Martha Couch Residence: Leslie County, Kentucky Age: 21 Number of Marriages: Blank Bride's POB: Perry County, Kentucky Bride's father POB: Blank Bride's mother POB: Blank Marriage Book 7, page 617

Groom: John Collins Residence: Leslie County, Kentucky Age: 29 Number of Marriages: Blank Occupation: Farmer Groom's POB: Clay County, Kentucky Groom's father POB: Blank Groom's mother POB: Blank
Date of marriage: 2 September 1889
Bride: Victory Browning Residence: Leslie County, Kentucky Age: 24
Number of Marriages: Blank Bride's POB: Perry County, Kentucky Bride's father POB: Harlan County, Kentucky Bride's mother POB: Harlan County, Kentucky Marriage Book 7, page 313

Groom: Robert Collins Residence: Leslie County, Kentucky Age: 50
Number of Marriages: 3 Occupation: Farmer Groom's POB: Clay County, Kentucky Groom's father POB: Campbell County, Tennessee Groom's mother POB: Lee County, Virginia
Date of marriage: 27 February 1888
Bride: Nancy Jane Hensley Residence: Leslie County, Kentucky Age: 50
Number of Marriages: 2 Bride's POB: Clay County, Kentucky Bride's

father POB: Bumkin County, North Carolina Bride's mother POB: Bumkin County, North Carolina Marriage Book 7, Page 209

Groom: Thomas Collins Residence: Leslie County, Kentucky Age: 22 Number of Marriages: Blank Occupation: Farmer Groom's POB: Clay County, Kentucky Groom's father POB: Tennessee Groom's mother POB: Clay County, Kentucky
Date of marriage: 14 June 1894
Bride: Mary Jane Fee Residence: Leslie County, Kentucky Age: 22 Number of Marriages: 1 Bride's POB: Clay County, Kentucky Bride's father POB: Harlan County, Kentucky Bride's mother POB: Blank Marriage Book 7, page 607

Groom: Ulysses G. Collins Residence: Leslie County, Kentucky Age: 21 Number of Marriages: Blank Occupation: Farmer Groom's POB: Clay County, Kentucky Groom's father POB: Clay County, Kentucky Groom's mother POB: Lee County, Virginia
Date of marriage: 24 September 1890
Bride: Tabitha Ellen Collins Residence: Leslie County, Kentucky Age: 21 Number of Marriages: Blank Bride's POB: Clay County, Kentucky Bride's father POB: Clay County, Kentucky Bride's mother POB: Perry County, Kentucky Marriage Book 7, page 397

Groom: Washington Collins Residence: Leslie County, Kentucky Age: 38 Number of Marriages: 1 Occupation: Farmer Groom's POB: Letcher County, Kentucky Groom's father POB: North Carolina Groom's mother POB: Blank
Date of marriage: 16 February 1886
Bride: Nancy Hensley Residence: Leslie County, Kentucky Age: 25 Number of Marriages: Blank Bride's POB: Clay County, Kentucky Bride's father POB: Blank Bride's mother POB: Blank Marriage Book 7, page 41

Groom: William Collins Residence: Leslie County, Kentucky Age: 21 Number of Marriages: Blank Occupation: Farmer Groom's POB: Clay County, Kentucky Groom's father POB: Blank Groom's mother POB: Blank
Date of marriage: 12 August 1886
Bride: Martha Sisemore Residence: Leslie County, Kentucky Age: 18 Number of Marriages: Blank Bride's POB: Clay County, Kentucky Bride's father POB: Clay County, Kentucky Bride's mother POB: Clay County, Kentucky
Remarks: Note in the record reads as follows: "August 11th, 1886. Mr. M. Howard. You will please issue a marriage license for William Collins and Martha. Signed: John Sizemore"

Marriage Book 7, Page 93

Groom: William Collins Residence: Leslie County, Kentucky Age: 20 Number of Marriages: Blank Occupation: Farmer Groom's POB: Clay County, Kentucky Groom's father POB: Clay County, Kentucky Groom's mother POB: Clay County, Kentucky
Date of marriage: 9 June 1892
Bride: Lucinda Collins Residence: Leslie County, Kentucky Age: 18 Number of Marriages: Blank Bride's POB: Clay County, Kentucky Bride's father POB: Clay County, Kentucky Bride's mother POB: Clay County, Kentucky Marriage Book 7, page 491

Groom: William Collins Residence: Leslie County, Kentucky Age: 25 Number of Marriages: Blank Occupation: Farmer Groom's POB: Clay County, Kentucky Groom's father POB: Blank Groom's mother POB: Blank
Date of marriage: 7 July 1893
Bride: Polly Wooton Residence: Leslie County, Kentucky Age: 21 Number of Marriages: Blank Bride's POB: Perry County, Kentucky Bride's father POB: Perry County, Kentucky Bride's mother POB: Perry County, Kentucky Marriage Book 7, page 561

Colwell

Groom: Nesbia Colwell Residence: Perry County, Kentucky Age: 21 Number of Marriages: Blank Occupation: Farmer Groom's POB: Perry County, Kentucky Groom's father POB: Perry County, Kentucky Groom's mother POB: Perry County, Kentucky
Date of marriage: 27 March 1889
Bride: Mary Jane Wooton Residence: Leslie County, Kentucky Age: 16 Number of Marriages: Blank Bride's POB: Perry County, Kentucky Bride's father POB: Perry County, Kentucky Bride's mother POB: Perry County, Kentucky Marriage Book 7, page 285

Combs

Groom: Andrew Combs Residence: Clay County, Kentucky Age: 22 Number of Marriages: Blank Occupation: Farmer Groom's POB: Clay County, Kentucky Groom's father POB: Perry County, Kentucky Groom's mother POB: Perry County, Kentucky
Date of marriage: 16 September 1889
Bride: Ellen Helton Residence: Clay County, Kentucky Age: 17 Number of Marriages: Blank Bride's POB: Clay County, Kentucky Bride's father POB: Harlan County, Kentucky Bride's mother POB: Clay County. Kentucky

Remarks: Note in the record reads as follows: "To any Clerk of Leslie County. This is to certify that I authorized you to let to give Andrew Combs license to marry Ellen Helton. Given under my hand this the 18th day of September 1889. Signed: Carter Helton."
Marriage Book 7, page 317

Groom: Jackson Combs Residence: Leslie County, Kentucky Age: 21 Number of Marriages: Blank Occupation: Farmer Groom's POB: Perry County, Kentucky Groom's father POB: Perry County, Kentucky Groom's mother POB: Perry County, Kentucky
Date of marriage: 16 June 1890
Bride: Sarah Combs Residence: Leslie County, Kentucky Age: 18 Number of Marriages: Blank Bride's POB: Perry County, Kentucky Bride's father POB: Perry County, Kentucky Bride's mother POB: Perry County, Kentucky Marriage Book 7, page 371

Groom: Jackson Combs Residence: Perry County, Kentucky Age: 23 Number of Marriages: Blank Occupation: Farmer Groom's POB: Perry County, Kentucky Groom's father POB: Perry County, Kentucky Groom's mother POB: Breathitt County, Kentucky
Date of marriage: 4 March 1889
Bride: Eliza Baker Residence: Leslie County, Kentucky Age: 15 Number of Marriages: Blank Bride's POB: Perry County, Kentucky Bride's father POB: Blank Bride's mother POB: Blank
Remarks: Note appears in the record as follows: "Mr. J. M. Howard. Give Jackson Combs marriage license to marry my girl, Eliza Baker. Given under my hand this March 1, 1889. Signed: William Baker. Signed: Joseph Miniard."
Marriage Book 7, page 273

Groom: Preston Combs Residence: Leslie County, Kentucky Age: 22 Number of Marriages: Blank Occupation: Farmer Groom's POB: Clay County, Kentucky Groom's father POB: Blank Groom's mother POB: Blank
Date of marriage: 11 January 1893
Bride: Ella Brown Residence: Leslie County, Kentucky Age: 15 Number of Marriages: Blank Bride's POB: Knox County, Kentucky Bride's father POB: Clay County, Kentucky Bride's mother POB: Knox County, Kentucky
Marriage Book 7, page 533

Coots

Groom: Ance Coots Residence: Leslie County, Kentucky Age: About 30 Number of Marriages: 4 Occupation: Farmer Groom's POB: Perry County Groom's father POB: Blank Groom's mother POB: Blank
Date of marriage: 21 November 1885
Bride: Annie Ingle Residence: Leslie County, Kentucky Age: 24 Number of Marriages: 1 Bride's POB: Perry County, Kentucky Bride's father POB: Perry County, Kentucky Bride's mother POB: Perry County, Kentucky
Remarks: Note in the record as follows: "Mr. Clerk. This is to certify that I authorize you to issue license to marry my daughter Polly Williams to William Cornett. Signed William Williams and Margaret Williams"
Marriage Book 7, Page 23

Groom: James H. Coots Residence: Leslie County, Kentucky Age: 21 Number of Marriages: Blank Occupation: Farmer Groom's POB: Perry County, Kentucky Groom's father POB: Lee County, Virginia Groom's mother POB: Lee County, Virginia
Date of marriage: 2 March 1887
Bride: Mary Jane Wilson Residence: Leslie County, Kentucky Age: 16 Number of Marriages: Blank Bride's POB: Perry County, Kentucky Bride's father POB: North Carolina Bride's mother POB: Perry County, Kentucky
Marriage Book 7, Page 129

Groom: Sylvester Coots Residence: Leslie County, Kentucky Age: 18 Number of Marriages: Blank Occupation: Farmer Groom's POB: Perry County, Kentucky Groom's father POB: Virginia Groom's mother POB: Letcher County, Kentucky
Date of marriage: 14 October 1891
Bride: Olley Hamilton Residence: Leslie County, Kentucky Age: 14 Number of Marriages: Blank Bride's POB: Scott County, Virginia Bride's father POB: Blank Bride's mother POB: Scott County, Virginia Marriage Book 7, page 447

Groom: William Coots Residence: Leslie County, Kentucky Age: 25 Number of Marriages: 2 Occupation: Farmer Groom's POB: Perry County, Kentucky Groom's father POB: Blank Groom's mother POB: Blank
Date of marriage: 6 September 1885
Bride: Maryan Coots Residence: Leslie County, Kentucky Age: 18 Number of Marriages: 1 Bride's POB: Perry County, Kentucky Bride's father POB: Virginia Bride's mother POB: Kentucky
Remarks: There is a note in the record that reads as follows: "September 5th, 1885. Mr. J. M. Howard. Dear Sir. You will please issue a marriage license to Maryan Coots and William Coots. Given under my hand, this the 5th day of September 1885. ATT: David Lewis His mark "X" James Coots
Marriage Book 7, page 17

Groom: William D. Coots Residence: Leslie County, Kentucky Age: 45
Number of Marriages: 1 Occupation: Farmer Groom's POB: Wise County,
Virginia Groom's father POB: Wise County, Virginia Groom's mother
POB: Wise County, Virginia
Date of marriage: 26 April 1887
Bride: Elizabeth Boggs Residence: Leslie County, Kentucky Age: 33
Number of Marriages: Blank Bride's POB: Kentucky Bride's father POB:
Virginia Bride's mother POB: Virginia Marriage Book 7, Page 141

Cornett

Groom: Fred Cornett Residence: Leslie County, Kentucky Age: 25 Number
of Marriages: Blank Occupation: Farmer Groom's POB: Perry County,
Kentucky Groom's father POB: Perry County, Kentucky Groom's mother
POB: Harlan County, Kentucky
Date of marriage: 23 December 1893
Bride: Rodslia Howard Residence: Leslie County, Kentucky Age: 16
Number of Marriages: Blank Bride's POB: Perry County, Kentucky Bride's
father POB: Harlan County, Kentucky Bride's mother POB: Perry County,
Kentucky Marriage Book 7, page 579

Groom: Granville Cornett Residence: Leslie County, Kentucky Age: 28
Number of Marriages: 1 Occupation: Farmer Groom's POB: Letcher
County, Kentucky Groom's father POB: Perry County, Kentucky Groom's
mother POB: Wise County, Virginia
Date of marriage: 24 September 1889
Bride: Jesevine Lewis Residence: Leslie County, Kentucky Age: 28 Number
of Marriages: 1 Bride's POB: Tennessee Bride's father POB: Blank Bride's
mother POB: Blank Marriage Book 7, page 323

Groom: Robert Cornett Residence: Leslie County, Kentucky Age: 22
Number of Marriages: Blank Occupation: Farmer Groom's POB: Perry
County, Kentucky Groom's father POB: Perry County, Kentucky Groom's
mother POB: Harlan County, Kentucky
Date of marriage: 2 November 1887
Bride: Martha Baker Residence: Leslie County, Kentucky Age: 21
Number of Marriages: Blank Bride's POB: Perry County, Kentucky Bride's
father POB: Perry County, Kentucky Bride's mother POB: Perry County,
Kentucky Marriage Book 7, Page 175

Groom: William Cornett Residence: Perry County, Kentucky Age: 22

Number of Marriages: Blank Occupation: Farmer Groom's POB: Perry County, Kentucky Groom's father POB: Perry County, Kentucky Groom's mother POB: Perry County, Kentucky
Date of marriage: 22 April 1886
Bride: Polly Williams Residence: Leslie County, Kentucky Age: 18 Number of Marriages: Blank Bride's POB: Perry County, Kentucky Bride's father POB: Blank Bride's mother POB: Blank Marriage Book 7, Page 59

Couch

Groom: A. B. Couch Residence: Leslie County, Kentucky Age: 22 Number of Marriages: Blank Occupation: Farmer Groom's POB: Clay County, Kentucky Groom's father POB: Blank Groom's mother POB: Blank
Date of marriage: 11 November 1891
Bride: Sally Ann Davidson Residence: Leslie County, Kentucky Age: 21 Number of Marriages: Blank Bride's POB: Clay County, Kentucky Bride's father POB: Blank Bride's mother POB: Blank Marriage Book 7, page 449

Groom: Anderson Couch Residence: Leslie County, Kentucky Age: 24 Number of Marriages: Blank Occupation: Farmer Groom's POB: Perry County, Kentucky Groom's father POB: Perry County, Kentucky Groom's mother POB: Perry County, Kentucky
Date of marriage: 6 August 1887
Bride: Sally Couch Residence: Leslie County, Kentucky Age: 21 Number of Marriages: Blank Bride's POB: Perry County, Kentucky Bride's father POB: Perry County, Kentucky Bride's mother POB: Perry County, Kentucky Marriage Book 7, Page 159

Groom: Felix Couch Residence: Leslie County Age: 18 Number of Marriages: Blank Occupation: Farmer Groom's POB: Clay County, Kentucky Groom's father POB: Blank Groom's mother POB: Blank
Date of marriage: 31 March 1887
Bride: Lucindia Lewis Residence: Leslie County, Kentucky Age: 17 Number of Marriages: Blank Bride's POB: Clay County, Kentucky Bride's father POB: Blank Bride's mother POB: Blank
Remarks: Note appears in the record as follows: "This March 31, 1887. Mr. County Court Clerk or Deputy. I authorized you to issue marriage license to my son Felix Couch and in doing so will oblige me. Signed; Her mark "X" Sara Napier"
Marriage Book 7, Page 137

Groom: Harrison Couch Residence: Perry County, Kentucky Age: 21 Number of Marriages: Blank Occupation: Farmer Groom's POB: Perry

County, Kentucky Groom's father POB: Blank Groom's mother POB: Blank
Date of marriage: 10 March 1890
Bride: Elizabeth Lewis Residence: Leslie County, Kentucky Age: 16 Number of Marriages: Blank Bride's POB: Perry County, Kentucky Bride's father POB: Perry County, Kentucky Bride's mother POB: Perry County, Kentucky
Remarks: The following note appears in the record: "Mr. J. M. Howard, Clerk of Leslie County Court. Please issue marriage license for Harrison Couch and my girl, Elizabeth Lewis to marry. This 10th day of March 1890. Signed: Juder Lewis."
Marriage Book 7, page 353

Groom: John Couch Residence: Leslie County, Kentucky Age: 21 Number of Marriages: Blank Occupation: Farmer Groom's POB: Clay County, Kentucky Groom's father POB: Clay County, Kentucky Groom's mother POB: Clay County, Kentucky
Date of marriage: 29 January 1891
Bride: Sarah Napier Residence: Leslie County, Kentucky Age: 26 Number of Marriages: Blank Bride's POB: Clay County, Kentucky Bride's father POB: Harlan County, Kentucky Bride's mother POB: Clay County, Kentucky Marriage Book 7, page 415

Groom: Wilkerson Couch Residence: Leslie County, Kentucky Age: 26 Number of Marriages: Blank Occupation: Farmer Groom's POB: Clay County, Kentucky Groom's father POB: Clay County, Kentucky Groom's mother POB: Clay County, Kentucky
Date of marriage: 24 March 1890
Bride: Polly Howard Residence: Leslie County, Kentucky Age: 22 Number of Marriages: Blank Bride's POB: Harlan County, Kentucky Bride's father POB: Blank Bride's mother POB: Blank
Remarks: The following note appears in the record: "March 23rd, 1890. Mr. J. M. Howard. Sir, please let Wilk Couch have license to marry Polly Howard for me. Yours truly. Signed: His mark "X" Jackson Howard."
Marriage Book 7, page 359

Groom: William Couch Residence: Leslie County, Kentucky Age: 18 Number of Marriages: Blank Occupation: Farmer Groom's POB: Clay County, Kentucky Groom's father POB: Clay County, Kentucky Groom's mother POB: Clay County, Kentucky
Date of marriage: 26 August 1886
Bride: Polly Jane Napier Residence: Leslie County, Kentucky Age: 17 Number of Marriages: Blank Bride's POB: Clay County, Kentucky Bride's

father POB: Clay County, Kentucky Bride's mother POB: Clay County, Kentucky

Remarks: Note in the record reads as follows: "August 24, 1886. Mr. Mat Howard. Please give William Couch license to marry Polly Jane Napier. Signed: E. Z. Napier /// Mat Howard give William Couch his license. Signed: John Couch"

Marriage Book 7, Page 97

Creech

Groom: J. M. Creech Residence: Hyden, Leslie County, Kentucky Age: 21 Number of Marriages: Blank Occupation: Clerk Groom's POB: Wise County, Virginia Groom's father POB: Harlan County, Kentucky Groom's mother POB: Harlan County, Kentucky

Date of marriage: 26 October 1889

Bride: Lucy J. Maggard Residence: Leslie County, Kentucky Age: 21 Number of Marriages: 1 Bride's POB: Laurel County, Kentucky Bride's father POB: Perry County, Kentucky Bride's mother POB: Clay County, Kentucky Marriage Book 7, page 331

Groom: James Creech Residence: Leslie County, Kentucky Age: 20 Number of Marriages: Blank Occupation: Farmer Groom's POB: Perry County, Kentucky Groom's father POB: Blank Groom's mother POB: Perry County, Kentucky

Date of marriage: 2 September 1889

Bride: Ellen Lewis Residence: Leslie County, Kentucky Age: 14 Number of Marriages: Blank Bride's POB: Perry County, Kentucky Bride's father POB: Blank Bride's mother POB: Blank

Remarks: Note in the record reads as follows: "August 26, 1889. Cutshin, Leslie County. Mr. Clerk. Please let James Creech and Ellen Lewis have their license. Signed John C. Lewis."

Marriage Book 7, page 311

Cress

Groom: John Cress Residence: Leslie County, Kentucky Age: 28 Number of Marriages: Blank Occupation: Farmer Groom's POB: Perry County, Kentucky Groom's father POB: Virginia Groom's mother POB: Virginia

Date of marriage: 31 May 1887

Bride: Nancy Napier Residence: Blank Age: 17 Number of Marriages: Blank Bride's POB: Perry County, Kentucky Bride's father POB: Clay County, Kentucky Bride's mother POB: Perry County, Kentucky Marriage Book 7, page 149

Groom: Levi Cress Residence: Leslie County, Kentucky Age: 20 Number of Marriages: Blank Occupation: Farmer Groom's POB: Perry County, Kentucky Groom's father POB: Virginia Groom's mother POB: Perry County, Kentucky
Date of marriage: 31 May 1887
Bride: Rachel Jane Napier Residence: Leslie County, Kentucky Age: 19 Number of Marriages: Blank Bride's POB: Perry County, Kentucky Bride's father POB: Clay County, Kentucky Bride's mother POB: Perry County, Kentucky
Remarks: Note appears in the record as follows: "Mr. J. M. Howard, Clark of Leslie County. Please to give Rachel Jane Napier marriage license. Signed Her mark "X" Vina Napier. Attest: signed Jeff Lewis, Attest: Ellicott Press."
Marriage Book 7, Page 151

Groom: William Cress Residence: Wise County, Virginia Age: Blank Number of Marriages: Blank Occupation: Wise County, Virginia Groom's POB: Blank Groom's father POB: Blank Groom's mother POB: Blank
Date of marriage: 29 March 1887
Bride: Lucindia Causey Residence: Leslie County, Kentucky Age: 17 Number of Marriages: Blank Bride's POB: Harlan County, Kentucky Bride's father POB: Harlan County, Kentucky Bride's mother POB: Blank
Remarks: Note appears in the record as follows: "Mr. Madison Howard. Sir, please to give Lucindy Causey license to marry William Cress. This the 28th day of March 1887. Signed C. B. Causey."
Marriage Book 7, page 135

Daniels

Groom: C. B. Daniels Residence: Hyden, Kentucky Age: 18 Number of Marriages: 1 Occupation: Logman Groom's POB: Breathitt County, Kentucky Groom's father POB: Blank Groom's mother POB: Blank
Date of marriage: 21 February 1893
Bride: Elizabeth Eversole Residence: Hyden, Kentucky Age: 18 Number of Marriages: 1 Bride's POB: Jasmine County, Kentucky Bride's father POB: Blank Bride's mother POB: Blank Marriage Book 7, page 539

Davidson

Groom: Frank Davidson Residence: Leslie County, Kentucky Age: 17 Number of Marriages: 1 Occupation: Farmer Groom's POB: Clay County, Kentucky Groom's father POB: Clay County, Kentucky Groom's mother POB: Clay County, Kentucky
Date of marriage: 19 December 1892

Bride: Emeriah Napier Residence: Leslie County, Kentucky Age: 18
Number of Marriages: 1 Bride's POB: Clay County, Kentucky Bride's
father POB: Clay County, Kentucky Bride's mother POB: Clay County,
Kentucky Marriage Book 7, page 527

Groom: Loyd Davidson Residence: Clay County, Kentucky Age: 16
Number of Marriages: 1 Occupation: Farmer Groom's POB: Clay County,
Kentucky Groom's father POB: Clay County, Kentucky Groom's mother
POB: Blank
Date of marriage: 2 March 1893
Bride: Sally Stidham Residence: Wooton Creek, Kentucky Age: 16 Number
of Marriages: 1 Bride's POB: Perry County, Kentucky Bride's father POB:
Blank Bride's mother POB: Blank
Remarks: The following note appears in the record: "June 4th day 1894. Mr.
J. M. Howard. Sir, Please send E. D. Lewis and Jan Collins the marriage
license through they are under age and we will send you the money by John
Woods. Please send them through by return mail. Yours truly. Signed W. L.
Roberts Signed: Fannie Roberts. // This February the 26th, 1893. I certify by
that he is his own agent from both of us. This given under my hand. Signed:
Hiram Davidson Signed: Bell Gerry Davidson. TO Loyd Davidson."
Marriage Book 7, page 541

Davis

Groom: Hiram B. Davis Residence: Harlan County, Kentucky Age: 21
Number of Marriages: Blank Occupation: Farmer Groom's POB: Harlan
County, Kentucky Groom's father POB: Blank Groom's mother POB:
Blank
Date of marriage: 8 March 1889
Bride: Sarah Ingle Residence: Leslie County, Kentucky Age: 17 Number of
Marriages: Blank Bride's POB: Perry County, Kentucky Bride's father
POB: Virginia Bride's mother POB: Virginia
Remarks: Note appears in the record as follows: "Mr. Mat Howard. Please
grant these parties license to be married, her mother having given her up to
be married to Hiram B. Davis. The girl's name is Miss Sarah Ingle, Yours.
Signed: Jane Ingle."
Marriage Book 7, page 275

Day

Groom: Henry Day Residence: Leslie County, Kentucky Age: 23 Number of
Marriages: Blank Occupation: Farmer Groom's POB: Blank Groom's father
POB: Blank Groom's mother POB: Blank
Date of marriage: 11 March 1889

Bride: Polly Sandlin Residence: Leslie County, Kentucky Age: 23 Number of Marriages: 1 Bride's POB: Blank Bride's father POB: Blank Bride's mother POB: Blank Marriage Book 7, page 277

Groom: W. H. Day Residence: Blank Age: Blank Number of Marriages: Blank Occupation: Blank Groom's POB: Blank Groom's father POB: Blank Groom's mother POB: Blank
Date of marriage: 31 December 1891
Bride: Elizabeth Jane Cornett Residence: Blank Age: Blank Number of Marriages: Blank Bride's POB: Blank Bride's father POB: Blank Bride's mother POB: Blank
Remarks: Marriage bond was completed along with marriage certificate.
Marriage Book 7, page 479

Dixon

Groom: John L. Dixon Residence: Leslie County, Kentucky Age: 27 Number of Marriages: 1 Occupation: Lawyer Groom's POB: Clay County, Kentucky Groom's father POB: Harlan County, Kentucky Groom's mother POB: Clay County, Kentucky
Date of marriage: 20 August 1887
Bride: Lethie Ann Stamper Residence: Leslie County, Kentucky Age: 18 Number of Marriages: Blank Bride's POB: Perry County, Kentucky Bride's father POB: Perry County, Kentucky Bride's mother POB: Perry County, Kentucky Marriage Book 7, page 161

Groom: Leander Dixon Residence: Hyden, Kentucky Age: 23 Number of Marriages: Blank Occupation: Farmer Groom's POB: Clay County, Kentucky Groom's father POB: Harlan County, Kentucky Groom's mother POB: Clay County, Kentucky
Date of marriage: 14 April 1894
Bride: Emily Asher Residence: Hyden, Kentucky Age: 21 Number of Marriages: 2 Bride's POB: Clay County, Kentucky Bride's father POB: Clay County, Kentucky Bride's mother POB: Harlan County, Kentucky
Remarks: Married at Susan Begley's home.
Marriage Book 7, page 601

Groom: William Dixon Residence: Leslie County, Kentucky Age: 30 Number of Marriages: Blank Occupation: Farmer Groom's POB: Perry County, Kentucky Groom's father POB: Harlan County, Kentucky Groom's mother POB: Clay County, Kentucky
Date of marriage: 12 September 1891
Bride: M. E. Napier Residence: Clay County, Kentucky Age: 20 Number of Marriages: Blank Bride's POB: Clay County, Kentucky Bride's father POB:

Clay County, Kentucky Bride's mother POB: Clay County, Kentucky
Marriage Book 7, page 441

Duff

Groom: Andrew Jackson Duff Residence: Leslie County, Kentucky Age: 19 Number of Marriages: Blank Occupation: Farmer Groom's POB: Clay County, Kentucky Groom's father POB: Knox County, Kentucky Groom's mother POB: Clay County, Kentucky
Date of marriage: 1 September 1886
Bride: Silvania Buckhead Residence: Leslie County, Kentucky Age: 19 Number of Marriages: Blank Bride's POB: Clay County, Kentucky Bride's father POB: Blank Bride's mother POB: Blank Marriage Book 7, page 103

Eastridge

Groom: F. G. Eastridge Residence: Leslie County, Kentucky Age: 21 Number of Marriages: Blank Occupation: Farmer Groom's POB: Perry County, Kentucky Groom's father POB: Perry County, Kentucky Groom's mother POB: Harlan County, Kentucky
Date of marriage: 23 December 1893
Bride: Serena Hoskins Residence: Leslie County, Kentucky Age: 18 Number of Marriages: Blank Bride's POB: Perry County, Kentucky Bride's father POB: Blank Bride's mother POB: Blank
Remarks: The following note appears in the record: "December 23, 1893. Mr. J. M. Howard. You will give F. G. Eastridge and Serena Hoskins marriage license. This given under my hand. Signed: Irvine Hoskins."
Marriage Book 7, page 577

Eldridge

Groom: William Eldridge Residence: Leslie County, Kentucky Age: 40 Number of Marriages: 1 Occupation: Farmer Groom's POB: Perry County, Kentucky Groom's father POB: Blank Groom's mother POB: Blank
Date of marriage: 9 November 1887
Bride: Manervy Roark Residence: Leslie County, Kentucky Age: 44 Number of Marriages: Blank Bride's POB: Blank Bride's father POB: Blank Bride's mother POB: Blank
Remarks: Note in the record reads as follows: "Mr. J. M. Howard. Dear Sir. You will please send me their license by Levi Lewis and I will pay you for them. Sincerely February 19th day 1887. Signed: David Y. Lewis."
Marriage Book 7, page 177

Eversole

Groom: Abner Eversole Residence: Leslie County, Kentucky Age: 26
Number of Marriages: Blank Occupation: Merchandizing Groom's POB:
Owsley County, Kentucky Groom's father POB: Perry County, Kentucky
Groom's mother POB: Clay County, Kentucky
Date of marriage: 24 December 1886
Bride: Elizabeth Napier Residence: Leslie County, Kentucky Age: 18
Number of Marriages: Blank Bride's POB: Perry County, Kentucky Bride's
father POB: Perry County, Kentucky Bride's mother POB: Perry County,
Kentucky Marriage Book 8, page 117

Groom: Alexander Eversole Residence: Leslie County, Kentucky Age: 22
Number of Marriages: Blank Occupation: Farmer Groom's POB: Perry
County, Kentucky Groom's father POB: Not known Groom's mother POB:
Not known
Date of marriage: 7 November 1890
Bride: Sarah Pennington Residence: Leslie County, Kentucky Age: 16
Number of Marriages: Blank Bride's POB: Perry County, Kentucky Bride's
father POB: Blank Bride's mother POB: Blank Marriage Book 7, page 405

Groom: J. M. Eversole Residence: Leslie County, Kentucky Age: 19
Number of Marriages: Blank Occupation: Merchant Groom's POB: Owsley
County, Kentucky Groom's father POB: Perry County, Kentucky Groom's
mother POB: Clay County, Kentucky
Date of marriage: 1 September 1889
Bride: Nancy J. Boggs Residence: Leslie County, Kentucky Age: 15
Number of Marriages: Blank Bride's POB: Perry County, Kentucky Bride's
father POB: Letcher County, Kentucky Bride's mother POB: Letcher
County, Kentucky Marriage Book 7, page 309

Groom: W. B. Eversole Residence: Hyden, Kentucky Age: 58 Number of
Marriages: 3 Occupation: Farmer and County Judge Groom's POB: Blank
Groom's father POB: Blank Groom's mother POB: Blank
Date of marriage: 11 June 1892
Bride: Susan Begley Residence: Mouth of Cutshin Creek, Leslie County,
Kentucky Age: Blank Number of Marriages: 2 Bride's POB: Blank Bride's
father POB: Blank Bride's mother POB: Blank
Remarks: Married at Hyden, Kentucky
Marriage Book 7, page 495

Farler

Groom: French Farler Residence: Coon Creek, Kentucky Age: 21 Number
of Marriages: 1 Occupation: Farmer Groom's POB: Harlan County,

Kentucky Groom's father POB: Harlan County, Kentucky Groom's mother POB: Harlan County, Kentucky
Date of marriage: 28 December 1893
Bride: Rachel Jane Cornett Residence: Leslie County, Kentucky Age: 17 Number of Marriages: 1 Bride's POB: Perry County, Kentucky Bride's father POB: Perry County, Kentucky Bride's mother POB: Virginia
Remarks: The following note appears in the record: "I hereby agree to give French Farler let to get license to marry my daughter, Rachel Jane Cornett. Signed: William Cornett."
Marriage Book 7, page 581

Farmer

Groom: John C. Farmer Residence: Hyden, Kentucky Age: Blank Number of Marriages: 1 Occupation: Attorney at law Groom's POB: Spruce River, Leslie County, Kentucky Groom's father POB: Blank Groom's mother POB: Blank
Date of marriage: 4 May 1893
Bride: Sarah J. Morgan Residence: Clay County, Kentucky Age: Blank Number of Marriages: 1 Bride's POB: Blank Bride's father POB: Blank Bride's mother POB: Blank
Remarks: Married at G. W. Morgan's residence.
Marriage Book 7, page 549

Groom: W. A. Farmer Residence: Leslie County, Kentucky Age: 23 Number of Marriages: 1 Occupation: Farmer Groom's POB: Clay County, Kentucky Groom's father POB: Clay County, Kentucky Groom's mother POB: Clay County, Kentucky
Date of marriage: 10 October 1891
Bride: Nancy Morgan Residence: Leslie County, Kentucky Age: 23 Number of Marriages: Blank Bride's POB: Clay County, Kentucky Bride's father POB: Clay County, Kentucky Bride's mother POB: Clay County, Kentucky
Remarks: Married in Judge Eversole's office. Minister was Rev. E. Hubbard.
Marriage Book 7, page 445

Fee

Groom: James L. Fee Residence: Harlan County, Kentucky Age: 21 Number of Marriages: Blank Occupation: Farmer Groom's POB: Harlan County, Kentucky Groom's father POB: Harlan County, Kentucky Groom's mother POB: Harlan County, Kentucky
Date of marriage: 17 December 1889

Bride: Mary Jane Howard Residence: Leslie County, Kentucky Age: 17 Number of Marriages: Blank Bride's POB: Perry County, Kentucky Bride's father POB: Harlan County, Kentucky Bride's mother POB: Perry County, Kentucky Marriage Book 7, page 347

Feltner

Groom: E. B. Feltner Residence: Leslie County, Kentucky Age: 21 Number of Marriages: Blank Occupation: Farmer Groom's POB: Perry County, Kentucky Groom's father POB: Perry County, Kentucky Groom's mother POB: Perry County, Kentucky
Date of marriage: 3 September 1888
Bride: Catherine Napier Residence: Leslie County, Kentucky Age: 18 Number of Marriages: 1 Bride's POB: Clay County, Kentucky Bride's father POB: Clay County, Kentucky Bride's mother POB: Clay County, Kentucky Marriage Book 7, page 237

Groom: Esaw Feltner Residence: Leslie County, Kentucky Age: 24 Number of Marriages: Blank Occupation: Farmer Groom's POB: Perry County, Kentucky Groom's father POB: Unknown Groom's mother POB: Unknown
Date of marriage: 12 October 1885
Bride: Margaret Lewis Residence: Leslie County, Kentucky Age: 15 Number of Marriages: Blank Bride's POB: Perry Count, Kentucky Bride's father POB: Harlan County, Kentucky Bride's mother POB: Harlan County, Kentucky
Remarks: Note in the record as follows: "Mr. J. M. Howard, County Clerk, Leslie County. Please let Esaw Feltner have license to marry my daughter Margie Lewis this the 12th day of October 1885. Signed: John Lewis."
Marriage Book 7, Page 19

Groom: Felix Feltner Residence: Leslie County, Kentucky Age: 29 Number of Marriages: 1 Occupation: Farmer Groom's POB: Perry County, Kentucky Groom's father POB: Perry County, Kentucky Groom's mother POB: Perry County, Kentucky
Date of marriage: 22 February 1889
Bride: Lucy Sisemore Residence: Leslie County, Kentucky Age: 18 Number of Marriages: Blank Bride's POB: Clay County, Kentucky Bride's father POB: Blank Bride's mother POB: Blank
Remarks: Note appears in the record as follows: "This February 20, 1889. This is to certify that Nancy Sisemore gives up her girl Lucy Sisemore to Felix Feltner to marry. Signed Nancy Sisemore. Attest: Nannie North."
Marriage Book 7, page 271

Groom: Harrison Feltner Residence: Leslie County, Kentucky Age: 22 Number of Marriages: Blank Occupation: Farmer Groom's POB: Perry County, Kentucky Groom's father POB: Perry County, Kentucky Groom's mother POB: Perry County, Kentucky
Date of marriage: 24 January 1894
Bride: Ellen Feltner Residence: Leslie County, Kentucky Age: 18 Number of Marriages: Blank Bride's POB: Perry County, Kentucky Bride's father POB: Perry County, Kentucky Bride's mother POB: Perry County, Kentucky Marriage Book 7, page 585

Groom: Jackson Feltner Residence: Leslie County, Kentucky Age: 24 Number of Marriages: 1 Occupation: Farmer Groom's POB: Perry County, Kentucky Groom's father POB: Perry County, Kentucky Groom's mother POB: Perry County, Kentucky Date of marriage: 4 March 1891
Bride: Sarah Bell Feltner Residence: Leslie County, Kentucky Age: 14 Number of Marriages: Blank Bride's POB: Perry County, Kentucky Bride's father POB: Perry County, Kentucky Bride's mother POB: Perry County, Kentucky Marriage Book 7, page 421

Groom: John Feltner Residence: Leslie County, Kentucky Age: 26 Number of Marriages: Blank Occupation: Farmer Groom's POB: Perry County, Kentucky Groom's father POB: Blank Groom's mother POB: Blank
Date of marriage: 17 September 1890
Bride: Jane Napier Residence: Leslie County, Kentucky Age: 16 Number of Marriages: Blank Bride's POB: Perry County, Kentucky Bride's father POB: Blank Bride's mother POB: Blank
Remarks: The following note appears in the record: "Mr. J. M. Howard. Please issue marriage license for John Feltner and Jane Napier. This September 14, 1890. Signed: H. N. Napier."
Marriage Book 7, page 391

Groom: John Feltner Residence: Perry County, Kentucky Age: 22 Number of Marriages: 1 Occupation: Farmer Groom's POB: Perry County, Kentucky Groom's father POB: Perry County, Kentucky Groom's mother POB: Perry County, Kentucky
Date of marriage: 9 February 1893
Bride: Sally Wooton Residence: Leslie County, Kentucky Age: 21 Number of Marriages: 1 Bride's POB: Perry County, Kentucky Bride's father POB: Perry County, Kentucky Bride's mother POB: Perry County, Kentucky
Marriage Book 7, page 535

Groom: M. B. Feltner Residence: Wooton's Creek, Kentucky Age: 21 Number of Marriages: 1 Occupation: Farmer Groom's POB: Perry County, Kentucky Groom's father POB: Blank Groom's mother POB: Blank

Date of marriage: 18 June 1893
Bride: Rebecca Napier Residence: Wooton's Creek, Kentucky Age: 14
Number of Marriages: 1 Bride's POB: Perry County, Kentucky Bride's
father POB: Blank Bride's mother POB: Blank
Remarks: Married at Wooton's Creek Schoolhouse.
Marriage Book 7, page 555

Groom: Madison Feltner Residence: Leslie County, Kentucky Age: 21
Number of Marriages: Blank Occupation: Farmer Groom's POB: Perry
County, Kentucky Groom's father POB: Perry County, Kentucky Groom's
mother POB: Perry County, Kentucky
Date of marriage: 16 March 1892
Bride: Judia Baker Residence: Leslie County, Kentucky Age: Blank
Number of Marriages: 1 Bride's POB: Perry County, Kentucky Bride's
father POB: Perry County, Kentucky Bride's mother POB: Perry County,
Kentucky Marriage Book 7, page 467

Groom: Madison Feltner Residence: Leslie County, Kentucky Age: 23
Number of Marriages: 1 Occupation: Farmer Groom's POB: Perry County,
Kentucky Groom's father POB: Blank Groom's mother POB: Blank
Date of marriage: 28 March 1894
Bride: Rilda Status Residence: Leslie County, Kentucky Age: 18 Number of
Marriages: Blank Bride's POB: Lee County, Virginia Bride's father POB:
Blank Bride's mother POB: Blank Marriage Book 7, page 595

Groom: N. B. Feltner Residence: Leslie County, Kentucky Age: 18 Number
of Marriages: Blank Occupation: Farmer Groom's POB: Perry County,
Kentucky Groom's father POB: Perry County, Kentucky Groom's mother
POB: Perry County, Kentucky
Date of marriage: 25 November 1889
Bride: Polly Hoskins Residence: Leslie County, Kentucky Age: 16 Number
of Marriages: Blank Bride's POB: Perry County, Kentucky Bride's father
POB: Perry County, Kentucky Bride's mother POB: Perry County,
Kentucky Marriage Book 7, page 335

Fields

Groom: Emanuel Fields Residence: Perry County, Kentucky Age: 16
Number of Marriages: Blank Occupation: Farmer Groom's POB: Perry
County, Kentucky Groom's father POB: Blank Groom's mother POB:
Blank
Date of marriage: 8 February 1893

Bride: Nancy Jane Stidham Residence: Leslie County, Kentucky Age: 15 Number of Marriages: Blank Bride's POB: Perry County, Kentucky Bride's father POB: Blank Bride's mother POB: Blank Marriage Book 7, page 537

Groom: William H. Fields Residence: Letcher County, Kentucky Age: 23 Number of Marriages: 1 Occupation: Farmer Groom's POB: Perry County, Kentucky Groom's father POB: Letcher County, Kentucky Groom's mother POB: Virginia
Date of marriage: 7 January 1888
Bride: Susannah Banks Residence: Letcher County, Kentucky Age: 23 Number of Marriages: Blank Bride's POB: Letcher County, Kentucky Bride's father POB: Letcher County, Kentucky Bride's mother POB: Letcher County, Kentucky Marriage Book 7, page 193

Flanery

Groom: William H. Flanery Residence: Letcher County, Kentucky Age: 23 Number of Marriages: 1 Occupation: Carpenter Groom's POB: Virginia Groom's father POB: Blank Groom's mother POB: Blank
Date of marriage: 7 October 1892
Bride: Judia Shepherd Residence: Leslie County, Kentucky Age: 19 Number of Marriages: 2 Bride's POB: Perry County, Kentucky Bride's father POB: Wise County, Virginia Bride's mother POB: Perry County, Kentucky Marriage Book 7, page 511

Gay

Groom: Elijah Gay Residence: Leslie County, Kentucky Age: 21 Number of Marriages: Blank Occupation: Farmer Groom's POB: Perry County, Kentucky Groom's father POB: Perry County, Kentucky Groom's mother POB: Perry County, Kentucky
Date of marriage: 14 July 1894
Bride: Susan Hensley Residence: Leslie County, Kentucky Age: 17 Number of Marriages: Blank Bride's POB: Clay County, Kentucky Bride's father POB: North Carolina Bride's mother POB: Clay County, Kentucky Marriage Book 7, page 619

Groom: John Gay Residence: Leslie County, Kentucky Age: 18 Number of Marriages: 1 Occupation: Farmer Groom's POB: Clay County, Kentucky Groom's father POB: Perry County, Kentucky Groom's mother POB: Clay County, Kentucky
Date of marriage: 13 October 1892
Bride: America Hensley Residence: Leslie County, Kentucky Age: 33 Number of Marriages: 2 Bride's POB: Clay County, Kentucky Bride's

father POB: Clay County, Kentucky Bride's mother POB: Blank Marriage Book 7, page 515

Groom: Nelson Gay Residence: Leslie County, Kentucky Age: 21 Number of Marriages: 1 Occupation: Farmer Groom's POB: Clay County, Kentucky Groom's father POB: Clay County, Kentucky Groom's mother POB: Clay County, Kentucky
Date of marriage: 8 April 1889
Bride: Martha Barger Residence: Clay County, Kentucky Age: 21 Number of Marriages: Blank Bride's POB: Clay County, Kentucky Bride's father POB: Perry County, Kentucky Bride's mother POB: Clay County, Kentucky
Remarks: Note appears in the record as follows: "April 7th, 1889. I hereby notify any clerk of Leslie County to issue marriage license between Nelson Gay and Martha Barger. Signed: Andrew Barger."
Marriage Book 7, page 289

Groom: William Gay Residence: Clay County, Kentucky Age: 22 Number of Marriages: Blank Occupation: Farmer Groom's POB: Clay County, Kentucky Groom's father POB: Harlan County, Kentucky Groom's mother POB: Clay County, Kentucky
Date of marriage: 23 January 1894
Bride: Jane Bishop Residence: Leslie County, Kentucky Age: 27 Number of Marriages: 1 Bride's POB: Owsley County, Kentucky Bride's father POB: Blank Bride's mother POB: Blank Marriage Book 7, page 583

Gibson

Groom: James Gibson Residence: Bull Skin, Leslie County, Kentucky Age: 18 Number of Marriages: 1 Occupation: Farmer Groom's POB: Clay County, Kentucky Groom's father POB: Scott County, Virginia Groom's mother POB: Clay County, Kentucky
Date of marriage: 18 September 1887
Bride: Betty Howard Residence: Clay County, Kentucky Age: 26 Number of Marriages: 1 Bride's POB: Clay County, Kentucky Bride's father POB: Not known Bride's mother POB: Not Known
Remarks: Married at school house on Bull Skin.
Marriage Book 7, page 165

Gilbert

Groom: Miller Gilbert Residence: Blank Age: Blank Number of Marriages: Blank Occupation: Blank Groom's POB: Blank Groom's father POB: Blank Groom's mother POB: Blank
Date of marriage: 28 March 1893

Bride: Catherine Hooker Residence: Blank Age: Blank Number of Marriages: Blank Bride's POB: Blank Bride's father POB: Blank Bride's mother POB: Blank
Remarks: Marriage bond complete but no marriage certificate.
Marriage Book 7, page 543

Griffitt

Groom: James Griffitt Residence: Perry County, Kentucky Age: 19 Number of Marriages: Blank Occupation: Farmer Groom's POB: Clay County, Kentucky Groom's father POB: Harlan County, Kentucky Groom's mother POB: Harlan County, Kentucky
Date of marriage: 17 March 1886
Bride: Jane Joseph Residence: Leslie County, Kentucky Age: 22 Number of Marriages: 1 Bride's POB: Perry County, Kentucky Bride's father POB: Virginia Bride's mother POB: Virginia
Remarks: Note in the record reads as follows: "Mr. Mat Howard. You will please give James Griffitt and Jan Joseph license. This the 17th day of March 1886. Signed: Jacob Griffitt."
Marriage Book 7, page 53

Gross

Groom: J. B. Gross, Jr. Residence: Clay County, Kentucky Age: 20 Number of Marriages: Blank Occupation: Farmer Groom's POB: Owsley County, Kentucky Groom's father POB: Harlan County, Kentucky Groom's mother POB: Harlan County, Kentucky
Date of marriage: 4 December 1889
Bride: Arrend Cope Residence: Leslie County, Kentucky Age: 16 Number of Marriages: Blank Bride's POB: Rockcastle County, Kentucky Bride's father POB: Tennessee Bride's mother POB: Madison County, Kentucky
Remarks: Note in the record reads as follows: "December the 4th, 1889. Mr. J. M. Howard or deputy. Sir. Please let J. B. Gross have a license to marry Arrend C. Cope and oblige, yours truly, Signed: J. B. Gross, Sr. Signed: Emmanuel Cope."
Marriage Book 7, page 343

Hacker

Groom: John Hacker Residence: Leslie County, Kentucky Age: 30 Number of Marriages: 1 Occupation: Farmer Groom's POB: Bell County, Kentucky Groom's father POB: Virginia Groom's mother POB: Tennessee
Date of marriage: 22 May 1886

Bride: Louisa Sisemore Residence: Leslie County, Kentucky Age: 18 Number of Marriages: Blank Bride's POB: Blank Bride's father POB: Blank Bride's mother POB: Blank Marriage Book 7, Page 69

Hast

Groom: E. L. Hast Residence: Leslie County, Kentucky Age: 22 Number of Marriages: Blank Occupation: Farmer Groom's POB: Letcher County, Kentucky Groom's father POB: Virginia Groom's mother POB: Virginia
Date of marriage: 4 August 1890
Bride: Olena Langdon Residence: Leslie County, Kentucky Age: 18 Number of Marriages: Blank Bride's POB: Perry County, Kentucky Bride's father POB: Blank Bride's mother POB: Blank Marriage Book 7, page 381

Hayes

Groom: Hiram H. Hayes Residence: Leslie County, Kentucky Age: 52 Number of Marriages: 1 Occupation: Merchant Groom's POB: Blank Groom's father POB: Blank Groom's mother POB: Blank
Date of marriage: 28 March 1891
Bride: Nancy Ann Griffitts Residence: Leslie County, Kentucky Age: 21 Number of Marriages: 1 Bride's POB: Perry County, Kentucky Bride's father POB: Harlan County, Kentucky Bride's mother POB: Perry County, Kentucky Marriage Book 7, page 423

Hazelwood

Groom: G. M. Hazelwood Residence: Clay County, Kentucky Age: 23 Number of Marriages: 1 Occupation: Farmer and school teacher Groom's POB: Clay County, Kentucky Groom's father POB: Madison County, Kentucky Groom's mother POB: Laurel County, Kentucky
Date of marriage: 8 October 1892
Bride: Rebecca Ellen Valentine Residence: Leslie County, Kentucky Age: 18 Number of Marriages: 1 Bride's POB: Perry County, Kentucky Bride's father POB: Clay County, Kentucky Bride's mother POB: Clay County, Kentucky Marriage Book 7, page 513

Henson

Groom: William Henson Residence: Clay County, Kentucky Age: 21 Number of Marriages: Blank Occupation: Farmer Groom's POB: Clay County, Kentucky Groom's father POB: Clay County, Kentucky Groom's mother POB: Clay County, Kentucky
Date of marriage: 19 June 1894

Bride: Annie Hoskins Residence: Leslie County, Kentucky Age: 20 Number of Marriages: Blank Bride's POB: Clay County, Kentucky Bride's father POB: Harlan County, Kentucky Bride's mother POB: Clay County, Kentucky Marriage Book 7, page 609

Herd

Groom: Jacob Herd Residence: Harlan County, Kentucky Age: 42 Number of Marriages: Blank Occupation: Farmer Groom's POB: Hawkins County, Tennessee Groom's father POB: North Carolina Groom's mother POB: Virginia
Date of marriage: 13 May 1886
Bride: Nancy Day Residence: Harlan County, Kentucky Age: 23 Number of Marriages: 1 Bride's POB: Lee County, Kentucky Bride's father POB: Blank Bride's mother POB: Blank Marriage Book 7, Page 65

Hibbard

Groom: Jackson Hibbard Residence: Perry County, Kentucky Age: 23 Number of Marriages: 1 Occupation: Lumberman Groom's POB: Clay County, Kentucky Groom's father POB: Clay County, Kentucky Groom's mother POB: Clay County, Kentucky
Date of marriage 16 February 1886:
Bride: Vina Jones Residence: Leslie County, Kentucky Age: 22 Number of Marriages: 2 Bride's POB: Clay County, Kentucky Bride's father POB: Clay County, Kentucky Bride's mother POB: Clay County, Kentucky Marriage Book 7, Page 205

Hignight

Groom: Elihu Hignight Residence: Leslie County, Kentucky Age: 22 Number of Marriages: Blank Occupation: Farmer Groom's POB: Perry County, Kentucky Groom's father POB: Blank Groom's mother POB: Blank
Date of marriage: 9 March 1894
Bride: Judia Baker Residence: Leslie County, Kentucky Age: 21 Number of Marriages: Blank Bride's POB: Perry County, Kentucky Bride's father POB: Blank Bride's mother POB: Blank Marriage Book 7, page 591

Holland

Groom: James C. Holland Residence: Clay County, Kentucky Age: 21 Number of Marriages: Blank Occupation: Farmer Groom's POB: Whitley

County, Kentucky Groom's father POB: Cherokee County, North Carolina Groom's mother POB: Whitley County, Kentucky
Date of marriage: 21 January 1891
Bride: Orlenia Couch Residence: Leslie County, Kentucky Age: 17 Number of Marriages: Blank Bride's POB: Perry County, Kentucky Bride's father POB: Perry County, Kentucky Bride's mother POB: Clay County, Kentucky Marriage Book 7, page 411

Hollen

Groom: Thomas Hollen Residence: Leslie County, Kentucky Age: 20 Number of Marriages: Blank Occupation: Farmer Groom's POB: Blank Groom's father POB: Blank Groom's mother POB: Blank
Date of marriage: 22 October 1894
Bride: Elizabeth Couch Residence: Blank Age: Blank Number of Marriages: Blank Bride's POB: Blank Bride's father POB: Blank Bride's mother POB: Blank Marriage Book 7, page 635

Hoskins

Groom: E. L. Hoskins Residence: Leslie County, Kentucky Age: 21 Number of Marriages: Blank Occupation: Farmer Groom's POB: Clay County, Kentucky Groom's father POB: Clay County, Kentucky Groom's mother POB: Jackson County, Kentucky
Date of marriage: 2 October 1889
Bride: Rebecca Jane Napier Residence: Leslie County, Kentucky Age: 28 Number of Marriages: 1 Bride's POB: Clay County, Kentucky Bride's father POB: Harlan County, Kentucky Bride's mother POB: Harlan County, Kentucky Marriage Book 7, page 329

Groom: Felix Hoskins Residence: Leslie County, Kentucky Age: 24 Number of Marriages: Blank Occupation: Farmer Groom's POB: Perry County, Kentucky Groom's father POB: Blank Groom's mother POB: Blank
Date of marriage: 4 August 1886
Bride: Lucy Morgan Residence: Leslie County, Kentucky Age: 19 Number of Marriages: Blank Bride's POB: Clay County, Kentucky Bride's father POB: Blank Bride's mother POB: Blank Marriage Book 7, page 85

Groom: H. C. Hoskins Residence: Clay County, Kentucky Age: 22 Number of Marriages: Blank Occupation: Farmer Groom's POB: Clay County, Kentucky Groom's father POB: Clay County, Kentucky Groom's mother POB: Clay County, Kentucky
Date of marriage: 7 September 1894

Bride: Emily Asher Residence: Whitley County, Kentucky Age: 21 Number of Marriages: Blank Bride's POB: Clay County, Kentucky Bride's father POB: Clay County, Kentucky Bride's mother POB: Clay County, Kentucky Marriage Book 7, page 631

Groom: Isaac Hoskins Residence: Leslie County, Kentucky Age: 18 Number of Marriages: Blank Occupation: Farmer Groom's POB: Clay County, Kentucky Groom's father POB: Clay County, Kentucky Groom's mother POB: Clay County, Kentucky
Date of marriage: 11 August 1886
Bride: Polly Bollin Residence: Leslie County, Kentucky Age: 20 Number of Marriages: Blank Bride's POB: Clay County, Kentucky Bride's father POB: Clay County, Kentucky Bride's mother POB: Clay County, Kentucky Remarks: Note in the record reads as follows: "August 11, 1886. J. M. Howard, Clerk. You will please grant my son, Isaac Hoskins married license and sent them by the bearer of this order and you will oblige me in so doing given under my had this 11th day of August 1886. Signed: His mark "X" John Hoskins."
Marriage Book 7, page 91

Groom: Russel Hoskins Residence: Leslie County, Kentucky Age: 18 Number of Marriages: 1 Occupation: Farmer Groom's POB: Perry County, Kentucky Groom's father POB: Perry County, Kentucky Groom's mother POB: Perry County, Kentucky
Date of marriage: 24 February 1888
Bride: Lisany Wooton Residence: Leslie County, Kentucky Age: 17 Number of Marriages: 1 Bride's POB: Perry County, Kentucky Bride's father POB: Perry County, Kentucky Bride's mother POB: Perry County, Kentucky Marriage Book 7, page 207

Groom: Russel Hoskins Residence: Leslie County, Kentucky Age: 20 Number of Marriages: Blank Occupation: Farmer Groom's POB: Perry County, Kentucky Groom's father POB: Blank Groom's mother POB: Perry County, Kentucky
Date of marriage: 12 July 1889
Bride: Rutha J. Lewis Residence: Leslie County, Kentucky Age: 18 Number of Marriages: Blank Bride's POB: Perry County, Kentucky Bride's father POB: Perry County, Kentucky Bride's mother POB: Perry County, Kentucky Marriage Book 7, page 299

Groom: William R. Hoskins Residence: Leslie County, Kentucky Age: 52 Number of Marriages: 2 Occupation: Doctor Groom's POB: Perry County, Kentucky Groom's father POB: Perry County, Kentucky Groom's mother POB: Perry County, Kentucky

Date of marriage: 20 June 1891
Bride: Rebecca Feltner Residence: Perry County, Kentucky Age: 45
Number of Marriages: 1 Bride's POB: Clay County, Kentucky Bride's father POB: Clay County, Kentucky Bride's mother POB: Clay County, Kentucky
Remarks: Married at W. D. Wooton's. Minister was William Stidham.
Marriage Book 7, page 431

Howard

Groom: Andrew Howard Residence: Leslie County, Kentucky Age: 42
Number of Marriages: 2 Occupation: Farmer Groom's POB: Harlan County, Kentucky Groom's father POB: Harlan County, Kentucky Groom's mother POB: Harlan County, Kentucky
Date of marriage: 2 April 1888
Bride: Jane Stidham Residence: Leslie County, Kentucky Age: 28 Number of Marriages: 2 Bride's POB: Tennessee Bride's father POB: Perry County, Kentucky Bride's mother POB: Perry County, Kentucky Marriage Book 7, page 215

Groom: David D. Howard Residence: Leslie County, Kentucky Age: 20
Number of Marriages: Blank Occupation: Farmer Groom's POB: Perry County, Kentucky Groom's father POB: Harlan County, Kentucky Groom's mother POB: Clay County, Kentucky
Date of marriage: 11 October 1888
Bride: Maryan Stidham Residence: Leslie County, Kentucky Age: 21
Number of Marriages: Blank Bride's POB: Perry County, Kentucky Bride's father POB: Perry County, Kentucky Bride's mother POB: Perry County, Kentucky Marriage Book 7, page 247

Groom: Felix Howard Residence: Leslie County, Kentucky Age: 16
Number of Marriages: 1 Occupation: Farmer Groom's POB: Hurricane, Leslie County, Kentucky Groom's father POB: Perry County, Kentucky Groom's mother POB: Perry County, Kentucky
Date of marriage: 14 July 1894
Bride: Katie Ford Residence: Cutshin, Leslie County, Kentucky Age: 21
Number of Marriages: 2 Bride's POB: Blank Bride's father POB: Perry County, Kentucky Bride's mother POB: Perry County, Kentucky
Remarks: Married at home of the bride.
Marriage Book 7, page 615

Groom: Henry J. Howard Residence: Leslie County, Kentucky Age: 22
Number of Marriages: Blank Occupation: Farmer Groom's POB: Perry

County, Kentucky Groom's father POB: Harlan County, Kentucky Groom's mother POB: Perry County, Kentucky
Date of marriage: 13 November 1889
Bride: Sarah J. Browning Residence: Leslie County, Kentucky Age: 18 Number of Marriages: Blank Bride's POB: Perry County, Kentucky Bride's father POB: Harlan County, Kentucky Bride's mother POB: Perry County, Kentucky
Remarks: Note appears in the record as follows: "October 4th, 1889. Mr. J. M. Howard. Sir, please issue H. J. Howard and Sarah J. Browning marriage license and oblige yours. Signed: Stephen Browning."
Marriage Book 7, page 333

Groom: James Howard Residence: Leslie County, Kentucky Age: 19
Number of Marriages: Blank Occupation: Farmer Groom's POB: Perry County, Kentucky Groom's father POB: Harlan County, Kentucky Groom's mother POB: Virginia
Date of marriage: 25 July 1894
Bride: Polly Baker Residence: Leslie County, Kentucky Age: 17 Number of Marriages: Blank Bride's POB: Perry County, Kentucky Bride's father POB: Perry County, Kentucky Bride's mother POB: Perry County, Kentucky Marriage Book 7, page 625

Groom: Isaac Howard Residence: Leslie County, Kentucky Age: 20
Number of Marriages: Blank Occupation: Farmer Groom's POB: Clay County, Kentucky Groom's father POB: Harlan County, Kentucky Groom's mother POB: Perry County, Kentucky
Date of marriage: 29 July 1890
Bride: Sarah Mosley Residence: Leslie County, Kentucky Age: 20 Number of Marriages: Blank Bride's POB: Clay County, Kentucky Bride's father POB: Blank Bride's mother POB: Blank
Remarks: The following note appears in the record: "July 28, 1890. Mr. J. M. Howard, Clerk of Leslie County Court. You will please give Isaac Howard marriage license to marry Sarah Mosley and this will be all right with me. Signed: Her mark "X" Samuel Mosley. Her mark "X" Sarah Mosley." // January 6, 1891. Mr. Madison Howard. You are hereby authorized to issue license for the marriage of Christopher Anderson. Signed: M. L. Anderson."
Marriage Book 7, page 377

Groom: Jesse Howard Residence: Leslie County, Kentucky Age: 20
Number of Marriages: Blank Occupation: Farmer Groom's POB: Clay County, Kentucky Groom's father POB: Harlan County, Kentucky Groom's mother POB: Clay County, Kentucky
Date of marriage: 10 March 1888

Bride: Elizabeth Asher Residence: Clay County, Kentucky Age: Blank Number of Marriages: Blank Bride's POB: Clay County, Kentucky Bride's father POB: Blank Bride's mother POB: Blank Marriage Book 7, page 211

Groom: John L. Howard Residence: Leslie County, Kentucky Age: 19 Number of Marriages: Blank Occupation: Farmer Groom's POB: Clay County, Kentucky Groom's father POB: Harlan County, Kentucky Groom's mother POB: Clay County, Kentucky
Date of marriage: 28 August 1886
Bride: Arra Sisemore Residence: Leslie County, Kentucky Age: 18 Number of Marriages: Blank Bride's POB: Clay County, Kentucky Bride's father POB: Clay County, Kentucky Bride's mother POB: Clay County, Kentucky
Remarks: Note in the record reads as follows: "Leslie County, Ky. This August 29th, 1886. This is stating that Blevins Sizemore give to John Howard Miss Array Sisemore his daughter from him. Signed: Blevins Sisemore."
Marriage Book 7, Page 101

Groom: Lee Howard Residence: Leslie County, Kentucky Age: 28 Number of Marriages: Blank Occupation: Farmer Groom's POB: Owsley County, Kentucky Groom's father POB: Harlan County, Kentucky Groom's mother POB: Perry County, Kentucky
Date of marriage: 20 September 1889
Bride: Susan Asher Residence: Leslie County, Kentucky Age: 28 Number of Marriages: Blank Bride's POB: Perry County, Kentucky Bride's father POB: Clay County, Kentucky Bride's mother POB: Harlan County, Kentucky
Remarks: Note in the record reads as follows: "To the Clerk of Leslie County Court. This is to certify that I have consented for you to issue marriage license to Sam Alfred Langdon and Susan Napier. This December 5th, 1891. Signed Simeon Langdon."
Marriage Book 7, page 321

Groom: Zachariah Howard Residence: Leslie County, Kentucky Age: 21 Number of Marriages: Blank Occupation: Farmer Groom's POB: Perry County, Kentucky Groom's father POB: Harlan County, Kentucky Groom's mother POB: Clay County, Kentucky
Date of marriage: 16 May 1887
Bride: Mary Asher Residence: Clay County, Kentucky Age: 21 Number of Marriages: Blank Bride's POB: Clay County, Kentucky Bride's father POB: Clay County, Kentucky Bride's mother POB: Clay County, Kentucky
Marriage Book 7, page 145

Huff

Groom: Simpson Huff Residence: Confluence, Kentucky Age: 21 Number of Marriages: Blank Occupation: Farmer Groom's POB: Perry County, Kentucky Groom's father POB: Perry County, Kentucky Groom's mother POB: Perry County, Kentucky
Date of marriage: 31 August 1894
Bride: Alpha Elizabeth Wooton Residence: Mad Dog, Kentucky Age: 20 Number of Marriages: Blank Bride's POB: Perry County, Kentucky Bride's father POB: Perry County, Kentucky Bride's mother POB: Perry County, Kentucky Marriage Book 7, page 627

Ingle

Groom: John Ingle Residence: Leslie County, Kentucky Age: 18 Number of Marriages: 1 Occupation: Farmer Groom's POB: Perry County, Kentucky Groom's father POB: Virginia Groom's mother POB: Virginia
Date of marriage: 16 February 1888
Bride: Sallie Baker Residence: Leslie County, Kentucky Age: 19 Number of Marriages: 1 Bride's POB: Perry County, Kentucky Bride's father POB: Perry County, Kentucky Bride's mother POB: Perry County, Kentucky
Remarks: Note appears in the record as follows: "This the 13th of February 1888. I give John Ingle leave to get license from any clerk of Leslie County to marry my girl. Signed: William Baker."
Marriage Book 7, Page 201

Groom: William Ingle Residence: Leslie County, Kentucky Age: 32 Number of Marriages: 2 Occupation: Farmer Groom's POB: Blank Groom's father POB: Blank Groom's mother POB: Blank
Date of marriage: 16 September 1889
Bride: Hannah Browning Residence: Leslie County, Kentucky Age: 34 Number of Marriages: 1 Bride's POB: Perry County, Kentucky Bride's father POB: Blank Bride's mother POB: Blank Marriage Book 7, page 315

Irvin

Groom: Ezekiel Irvin Residence: Leslie County, Kentucky Age: 21 Number of Marriages: Blank Occupation: Farmer Groom's POB: Harlan County, Kentucky Groom's father POB: Harlan County, Kentucky Groom's mother POB: Harlan County, Kentucky
Date of marriage: 30 November 1885
Bride: Elizabeth Pennington Residence: Leslie County, Kentucky Age: 20 Number of Marriages: Blank Bride's POB: Harlan County, Kentucky

Bride's father POB: Harlan County, Kentucky Bride's mother POB: Harlan County, Kentucky Marriage Book 7, Page 27

Johnson

Groom: Joseph Johnson Residence: Leslie County, Kentucky Age: 16 Number of Marriages: Blank Occupation: Farmer Groom's POB: Scott County, Virginia Groom's father POB: North Carolina Groom's mother POB: Kentucky
Date of marriage: 24 April 1887
Bride: Elizabeth Pennington Residence: Leslie County, Kentucky Age: 17 Number of Marriages: Blank Bride's POB: Kentucky Bride's father POB: Blank Bride's mother POB: Blank
Remarks: Note appears in the record as follows: " This the 22 day of April 1887. I do agree for Joseph Johnson and my daughter Mary E. Pennington her age in 17 in June. Signed: Jesse Pennington"
Marriage Book 7, page 139

Jones

Groom: Edmon Jones Residence: Leslie County, Kentucky Age: 22 Number of Marriages: Blank Occupation: Farmer Groom's POB: Clay County, Kentucky Groom's father POB: Clay County, Kentucky Groom's mother POB: Clay County, Kentucky
Date of marriage: 3 January 1888
Bride: Rachel Asburn Residence: Leslie County, Kentucky Age: 23 Number of Marriages: Blank Bride's POB: Clay County, Kentucky Bride's father POB: Clay County, Kentucky Bride's mother POB: Clay County, Kentucky Marriage Book 7, Page 191

Groom: Harvey Jones Residence: Leslie County, Kentucky Age: 21 Number of Marriages: Blank Occupation: Farmer Groom's POB: Clay County, Kentucky Groom's father POB: Clay County, Kentucky Groom's mother POB: Harlan County, Kentucky
Date of marriage: 8 April 1890
Bride: Polly Ann Asher Residence: Leslie County, Kentucky Age: 18 Number of Marriages: Blank Bride's POB: Clay County, Kentucky Bride's father POB: Blank Bride's mother POB: Clay County, Kentucky
Remarks: The following note appears in the record: "Mr. J. M. Howard, Clerk of Leslie County Court. Please give Harvey Jones and my girl, Polly Ann License to marry and oblige. This 8th day of April 1890. Signed: Her mark "X" Judia Asher."
Marriage Book 7, page 361

Groom: Hughes Jones Residence: Leslie County, Kentucky Age: 20 Number of Marriages: Blank Occupation: Farmer Groom's POB: Clay County, Kentucky Groom's father POB: Blank Groom's mother POB: Blank
Date of marriage: 16 October 1889
Bride: Eliza Wooton Residence: Leslie County, Kentucky Age: 16 Number of Marriages: Blank Bride's POB: Clay County, Kentucky Bride's father POB: Blank Bride's mother POB: Blank Marriage Book 7, page 327

Groom: Irvin Jones Residence: Leslie County, Kentucky Age: 18 Number of Marriages: Blank Occupation: Farmer Groom's POB: Perry County, Kentucky Groom's father POB: Blank Groom's mother POB: Blank
Date of marriage: 3 August 1887
Bride: Mary Elizabeth Jones Residence: Leslie County, Kentucky Age: 25 Number of Marriages: 1 Bride's POB: Virginia Bride's father POB: Virginia Bride's mother POB: Virginia Marriage Book 7, page 157

Groom: William Jones Residence: Leslie County, Kentucky Age: 18 Number of Marriages: Blank Occupation: Farmer Groom's POB: Clay County, Kentucky Groom's father POB: Clay County, Kentucky Groom's mother POB: Clay County, Kentucky
Date of marriage: 5 August 1886
Bride: Mary Sisemore Residence: Leslie County, Kentucky Age: 15 Number of Marriages: Blank Bride's POB: Clay County, Kentucky Bride's father POB: Clay County, Kentucky Bride's mother POB: Unknown Marriage Book 7, Page 87

Joseph

Groom: Reason Joseph Residence: Leslie County, Kentucky Age: 55 Number of Marriages: 2 Occupation: Farmer Groom's POB: Blank Groom's father POB: Blank Groom's mother POB: Blank
Date of marriage: 17 February 1891
Bride: Rosannah Pennington Residence: Leslie County, Kentucky Age: 35 Number of Marriages: 1 Bride's POB: Perry County, Kentucky Bride's father POB: Blank Bride's mother POB: Blank Marriage Book 7, page 419

Kennedy

Groom: John Kennedy Residence: Blank Age: Blank Number of Marriages: Blank Occupation: Blank Groom's POB: Blank Groom's father POB: Blank Groom's mother POB: Blank
Date of marriage: 31 December 1891

Bride: Julia A. Cope Residence: Blank Age: Blank Number of Marriages: Blank Bride's POB: Blank Bride's father POB: Blank Bride's mother POB: Blank
Remarks: Marriage bond was completed along with marriage certificate.
Marriage Book 7, page 475

Kilburn

Groom: John Kilburn Residence: Leslie County, Kentucky Age: 22 Number of Marriages: Blank Occupation: Farmer Groom's POB: Perry County, Kentucky Groom's father POB: Virginia Groom's mother POB: Perry County, Kentucky
Date of marriage: 17 March 1887
Bride: Judia Williams Residence: Leslie County, Kentucky Age: 17 Number of Marriages: Blank Bride's POB: Perry County, Kentucky Bride's father POB: Perry County, Kentucky Bride's mother POB: Virginia
Remarks: Note in the record appears as follows: "Mr. Clerk. Let John Kilburn have license to marry Juda Williams for I am willing. Signed Nathaniel Williams this the 12th day of March 1887."
Marriage Book 7, page 131

Langdon

Groom: Alfred Langdon Residence: Clay County, Kentucky Age: 19 Number of Marriages: Blank Occupation: Farmer Groom's POB: Perry County, Kentucky Groom's father POB: Perry County, Kentucky Groom's mother POB: Perry County, Kentucky
Date of marriage: 8 December 1891
Bride: Kissie Napier Residence: Clay County, Kentucky Age: 18 Number of Marriages: Blank Bride's POB: Clay County, Kentucky Bride's father POB: Clay County, Kentucky Bride's mother POB: Clay County, Kentucky
Marriage Book 7, page 461

Lewis

Groom: A. C. Lewis Residence: Clay County, Kentucky Age: 19 Number of Marriages: Blank Occupation: Merchant Groom's POB: Clay County, Kentucky Groom's father POB: Blank Groom's mother POB: Blank
Date of marriage: 1 October 1889
Bride: Arpha Farmer Residence: Leslie County, Kentucky Age: 18 Number of Marriages: Blank Bride's POB: Clay County, Kentucky Bride's father POB: Blank Bride's mother POB: Blank
Remarks: Note appears in the record as follows: "September 28, 1889. I the under signed authorize the county court clerk of any of his deputies to issue

marriage license for my son, A. C. Lewis. Signed Rebecca Wilson. // I the undersigned authorized the county clerk or any of his deputies to issue marriage license to my daughter, Arpha Farmer to A. C. Lewis. October 1. Signed H. J. Farmer."
Marriage Book 7, page 325

Groom: Abner Lewis Residence: Leslie County, Kentucky Age: 20 Number of Marriages: Blank Occupation: Farmer Groom's POB: Harlan County, Kentucky Groom's father POB: Harlan County, Kentucky Groom's mother POB: Harlan County, Kentucky
Date of marriage: 14 April 1894
Bride: Sarah Lewis Residence: Leslie County, Kentucky Age: 21 Number of Marriages: 1 Bride's POB: Perry County, Kentucky Bride's father POB: Blank Bride's mother POB: Blank Marriage Book 7, page 597

Groom: Daniel Lewis Residence: Leslie County, Kentucky Age: 53 Number of Marriages: 3 Occupation: Farmer Groom's POB: Perry County, Kentucky Groom's father POB: Perry County, Kentucky Groom's mother POB: Harlan County, Kentucky
Date of marriage: 3 May 1890
Bride: Peggie Couch Residence: Leslie County, Kentucky Age: 45 Number of Marriages: Blank Bride's POB: Clay County, Kentucky Bride's father POB: Blank Bride's mother POB: Blank Marriage Book 7, page 369

Groom: E. L. Lewis Residence: Leslie County, Kentucky Age: 20 Number of Marriages: Blank Occupation: Merchant Groom's POB: Clay County, Kentucky Groom's father POB: Clay County, Kentucky Groom's mother POB: Harlan County, Kentucky
Date of marriage: 19 September 1889
Bride: Martha J. Daniel Residence: Leslie County, Kentucky Age: 14 Number of Marriages: Blank Bride's POB: Breathitt County, Kentucky Bride's father POB: Clay County, Kentucky Bride's mother POB: Breathitt County, Kentucky
Remarks: Note in the record reads a follows: "Hyden, Kentucky. September 19th, 1889. This is to certify that E. L. Lewis is authorized by his father to marry Martha J. Daniel. Signed: John Lewis. Signed: Fannie Lewis."
Marriage Book 7, page 319

Groom: Harrison Lewis Residence: Leslie County, Kentucky Age: 23 Number of Marriages: Blank Occupation: Farmer Groom's POB: Perry County, Kentucky Groom's father POB: Blank Groom's mother POB: Blank
Date of marriage: 9 November 1888

Bride: Lucindia Pennington Residence: Leslie County, Kentucky Age: 28 Number of Marriages: 1 Bride's POB: Blank Bride's father POB: Blank Bride's mother POB: Blank Marriage Book 7, page 249

Groom: Henry D. Lewis Residence: Leslie County, Kentucky Age: 25 Number of Marriages: Blank Occupation: Farmer Groom's POB: Clay County, Kentucky Groom's father POB: Blank Groom's mother POB: Blank
Date of marriage: 28 May 1886
Bride: Lizzie Roberts Residence: Leslie County, Kentucky Age: 14 Number of Marriages: Blank Bride's POB: Clay County, Kentucky Bride's father POB: Blank Bride's mother POB: Blank
Remarks: Note in the record reads as follows: "Hyden, Leslie County, Kentucky. May 28, 1886. Mr. Howard. Please let H. D. Lewis and Lizzie Roberts have license to marry by my request. Signed: Martha Roberts."
Marriage Book 7, page 71

Groom: Ira Lewis Residence: Leslie County, Kentucky Age: 64 Number of Marriages: 1 Occupation: Farmer Groom's POB: Virginia Groom's father POB: Blank Groom's mother POB: Blank
Date of marriage: 22 May 1886
Bride: Jane Thomas Residence: Leslie County, Kentucky Age: 54 Number of Marriages: 1 Bride's POB: Blank Bride's father POB: Blank Bride's mother POB: Blank Marriage Book 7, page 67

Groom: J. H. Lewis Residence: Leslie County, Kentucky Age: 21 Number of Marriages: Blank Occupation: Mechanic Groom's POB: Perry County, Kentucky Groom's father POB: Perry County, Kentucky Groom's mother POB: Perry County, Kentucky
Date of marriage: 28 November 1891
Bride: Lilly Begley Residence: Leslie County, Kentucky Age: 16 Number of Marriages: Blank Bride's POB: Clay County, Kentucky Bride's father POB: Letcher County, Kentucky Bride's mother POB: Clay County, Kentucky
Marriage Book 7, page 457

Groom: James Lewis Residence: Leslie County, Kentucky Age: 18 Number of Marriages: 1 Occupation: Farmer Groom's POB: Perry County, Kentucky Groom's father POB: Perry County, Kentucky Groom's mother POB: Perry County, Kentucky
Date of marriage: 27 December 1887
Bride: Elizabeth Lewis Residence: Leslie County, Kentucky Age: 15 Number of Marriages: 1 Bride's POB: Perry County, Kentucky Bride's father POB: Perry County, Kentucky Bride's mother POB: Perry County, Kentucky Marriage Book 7, page 185

Groom: James L. Lewis Residence: Leslie County, Kentucky Age: 27 Number of Marriages: Blank Occupation: Farmer Groom's POB: Clay County, Kentucky Groom's father POB: Blank Groom's mother POB: Blank
Date of marriage: 5 October 1891
Bride: Martha Begley Residence: Blank Age: Blank Number of Marriages: Blank Bride's POB: Blank Bride's father POB: Blank Bride's mother POB: Blank
Remarks: Marriage bond was completed but the remainder of the license was not.
Marriage Book 7, page 443

Groom: John Lewis Residence: Leslie County, Kentucky Age: 24 Number of Marriages: Blank Occupation: Farmer Groom's POB: Perry County, Kentucky Groom's father POB: Perry County, Kentucky Groom's mother POB: Clay County, Kentucky
Date of marriage: 19 July 1890
Bride: Nancy France Residence: Leslie Country, Kentucky Age: 20 Number of Marriages: Blank Bride's POB: Perry County, Kentucky Bride's father POB: Perry County, Kentucky Bride's mother POB: Perry County, Kentucky
Remarks: The following note appears in the record: "Mr. J. M. Howard, Clerk of Leslie County Court. Please let John Lewis and my girl, Nancy France have license top marry. This 18th day of July 1890. Signed: Hansford France."
Marriage Book 7, page 375

Groom: R. J. Lewis Residence: Leslie County, Kentucky Age: 34 Number of Marriages: Blank Occupation: Framer Groom's POB: Perry County, Kentucky Groom's father POB: Blank Groom's mother POB: Harlan County, Kentucky
Date of marriage: 17 January 1889
Bride: Fannie Morgan Residence: Leslie County, Kentucky Age: 26 Number of Marriages: Blank Bride's POB: Blank Bride's father POB: Blank Bride's mother POB: Blank Marriage Book 7, page 261

Groom: S. J. Lewis Residence: Blank Age: Blank Number of Marriages: Blank Occupation: Blank Groom's POB: Blank Groom's father POB: Blank Groom's mother POB: Blank
Date of marriage: 11 August 1892
Bride: Martha Morgan Residence: Blank Age: Blank Number of Marriages: Blank Bride's POB: Blank Bride's father POB: Blank Bride's mother POB: Blank

Remarks: Marriage bond completed but no marriage certificate.
Marriage Book 7, page 503

Groom: Samuel Lewis Residence: Leslie County, Kentucky Age: 22 Number of Marriages: Blank Occupation: Farmer Groom's POB: Perry County, Kentucky Groom's father POB: Perry County, Kentucky Groom's mother POB: Perry County, Kentucky
Date of marriage: 8 August 1888
Bride: Lucindia Feltner Residence: Leslie County, Kentucky Age: 18 Number of Marriages: Blank Bride's POB: Perry County, Kentucky Bride's father POB: Perry County, Kentucky Bride's mother POB: Perry County, Kentucky Marriage Book 7, page 235

Groom: Samuel Lewis Residence: Leslie County, Kentucky Age: 58 Number of Marriages: 1 Occupation: Farmer Groom's POB: Perry County, Kentucky Groom's father POB: North Carolina Groom's mother POB: Blank
Date of marriage: 9 September 1891
Bride: Sarah Stidham Residence: Leslie County, Kentucky Age: 35 Number of Marriages: Blank Bride's POB: Perry County, Kentucky Bride's father POB: Perry County, Kentucky Bride's mother POB: Perry County, Kentucky Marriage Book 7, page 439

Groom: William Lewis Residence: Leslie County, Kentucky Age: 21 Number of Marriages: Blank Occupation: Farmer Groom's POB: Perry County, Kentucky Groom's father POB: Perry County, Kentucky Groom's mother POB: Clay County, Kentucky
Date of marriage: 5 July 1889
Bride: Sallie Fields Residence: Perry County, Kentucky Age: 22 Number of Marriages: Blank Bride's POB: Clay County, Kentucky Bride's father POB: Jackson County, Kentucky Bride's mother POB: Perry County, Kentucky Marriage Book 7, page 297

Groom: William Lewis Residence: Hyden, Kentucky Age: 21
Number of Marriages: Blank Occupation: Farmer Groom's POB: Perry County, Kentucky Groom's father POB: Perry County, Kentucky Groom's mother POB: Perry County, Kentucky
Date of marriage: 26 November 1889
Bride: Sally Ann Fields Residence: Perry County, Kentucky Age: 21 Number of Marriages: 1 Bride's POB: Perry County, Kentucky Bride's father POB: Perry County, Kentucky Bride's mother POB: Perry County, Kentucky Marriage Book 7, page 341

Groom: William Lewis Residence: Leslie County, Kentucky Age: 24
Number of Marriages: 1 Occupation: Farmer Groom's POB: Tennessee
Groom's father POB: Blank Groom's mother POB: Perry County, Kentucky
Date of marriage: 23 June 1893
Bride: Sylvania Hacker Residence: Leslie County, Kentucky Age: 21
Number of Marriages: Blank Bride's POB: Owsley County, Kentucky
Bride's father POB: Blank Bride's mother POB: Blank Marriage Book 7, page 557

Groom: William Lewis Residence: Leslie County, Kentucky Age: 25
Number of Marriages: Blank Occupation: Farmer and school teacher
Groom's POB: Perry County, Kentucky Groom's father POB: Perry County, Kentucky Groom's mother POB: Perry County, Kentucky
Date of marriage: 9 November 1893
Bride: Alice Morgan Residence: Leslie County, Kentucky Age: 18 Number of Marriages: Blank Bride's POB: Perry County, Kentucky Bride's father POB: Perry County, Kentucky Bride's mother POB: Perry County, Kentucky
Remarks: The following note appears in the record: "Mr. J. M. Howard. I hereby give my consent to the marriage of Miss Alice Morgan and William Lewis. November 9, 1983. Signed: A. B. Morgan."
Marriage Book 7, page 573

Maggard

Groom: A. B. Maggard Residence: Leslie County, Kentucky Age: 19
Number of Marriages: Blank Occupation: Farmer Groom's POB: Clay County, Kentucky Groom's father POB: Letcher County, Kentucky
Groom's mother POB: Perry County, Kentucky
Date of marriage: 24 February 1886
Bride: Lucy Eversole Residence: Leslie County, Kentucky Age: 18
Number of Marriages: Blank Bride's POB: Laurel County, Kentucky
Bride's father POB: Owsley County, Kentucky Bride's mother POB: Clay County, Kentucky Marriage Book 7, page 45

Groom: A. J. Maggard Residence: Letcher County, Kentucky Age: 25
Number of Marriages: Blank Occupation: Farmer Groom's POB: Letcher County, Kentucky Groom's father POB: Letcher County, Kentucky
Groom's mother POB: Letcher County, Kentucky
Date of marriage: 21 February 1894
Bride: Dora Jane Hart Residence: Leslie County, Kentucky Age: 18 Number of Marriages: Blank Bride's POB: Perry County, Kentucky Bride's father POB: Blank Bride's mother POB: Blank Marriage Book 7, page 587

Groom: Israel Maggard Residence: Leslie County, Kentucky Age: 35
Number of Marriages: 1 Occupation: Farmer Groom's POB: Perry County, Kentucky Groom's father POB: Letcher County, Kentucky Groom's mother POB: Harlan County, Kentucky
Date of marriage: 13 September 1890
Bride: Cassie Kilbourn Residence: Leslie County, Kentucky Age: 21
Number of Marriages: Blank Bride's POB: Blank Bride's father POB: Blank Bride's mother POB: Blank Marriage Book 7, page 389

Groom: Reuben Maggard Residence: Leslie County, Kentucky Age: 25
Number of Marriages: Blank Occupation: Farmer Groom's POB: Perry County, Kentucky Groom's father POB: Letcher County, Kentucky Groom's mother POB: Perry County, Kentucky
Date of marriage: 29 July 1885
Bride: Luvina Clark Residence: Leslie County, Kentucky Age: 22 Number of Marriages: Blank Bride's POB: Jackson County, Kentucky Bride's father POB: Blank Bride's mother POB: Blank
Remarks: Married at mouth of Coon Creek, Leslie County, Kentucky
Marriage Book 7, Page 11

Groom: W. R. Maggard Residence: Blank Age: Blank Number of Marriages: Blank Occupation: Blank Groom's POB: Blank Groom's father POB: Blank Groom's mother POB: Blank
Date of marriage: 4 November 1894
Bride: E. J. Vanover Residence: Blank Age: Blank Number of Marriages: Blank Bride's POB: Blank Bride's father POB: Blank Bride's mother POB: Blank Marriage Book 7, page 639

Groom: William Maggard Residence: Leslie County, Kentucky Age: 17
Number of Marriages: Blank Occupation: Farmer Groom's POB: Perry County, Kentucky Groom's father POB: Letcher County, Kentucky Groom's mother POB: Harlan County, Kentucky
Date of marriage: 5 May 1888
Bride: Alice Wooton Residence: Leslie County, Kentucky Age: 14
Number of Marriages: Blank Bride's POB: Perry County, Kentucky Bride's father POB: Perry County, Kentucky Bride's mother POB: Perry County, Kentucky
Remarks: Note in the record reads as follows: "May4, 1888. Mr. J. M. Howard. You can issue license for W. J. Maggard and Alice E. Wooton as far as I am concerned. Signed: Jackson Wooton //Mr. J. M. Howard. You can issue license for W. J. Maggard and Alice Wooton as far as I am concerned. Signed: John A. Maggard."
Marriage Book 7, Page 227

McCollum

Groom: Willis McCollum Residence: Clay County, Kentucky Age: 28 Number of Marriages: Blank Occupation: Farmer Groom's POB: Clay County, Kentucky Groom's father POB: Clay County, Kentucky Groom's mother POB: Clay County, Kentucky
Date of marriage: 29 August 1893
Bride: Rebecca Napier Residence: Clay County, Kentucky Age: 16 Number of Marriages: Blank Bride's POB: Clay County, Kentucky Bride's father POB: Clay County, Kentucky Bride's mother POB: Clay County, Kentucky
Remarks: The following note appears in the record: "March 2nd, 1891. This is to show that I authorize the Clerk of Leslie County to grant a marriage license between my daughter, Sarah Bell Feltner, and Jackson Feltner. Signed: Russel Feltner."
Marriage Book 7, page 563

McDaniel

Groom: Daniel McDaniel Residence: Leslie County, Kentucky Age: 28 Number of Marriages: 1 Occupation: Merchandising Groom's POB: Breathitt County, Kentucky Groom's father POB: Blank Groom's mother POB: Blank
Date of marriage: 29 November 1891
Bride: Rhoda Melton Residence: Leslie County, Kentucky Age: 20 Number of Marriages: Blank Bride's POB: Perry County, Kentucky Bride's father POB: Blank Bride's mother POB: Perry County, Kentucky Marriage Book 7, page 459

McKenney

Groom: Richard McKenney Residence: Leslie County, Kentucky Age: 25 Number of Marriages: 1 Occupation: Farmer Groom's POB: Clay County, Kentucky Groom's father POB: Lee County, Virginia Groom's mother POB: Lee County, Virginia
Date of marriage: 25 December 1891
Bride: Charlotte Boggs Residence: Leslie County, Kentucky Age: 18 Number of Marriages: Blank Bride's POB: Letcher County, Kentucky Bride's father POB: Blank Bride's mother POB: Blank Marriage Book 7, page 463

McKinney

Groom: Daniel McKinney Residence: Leslie County, Kentucky Age: 67 Number of Marriages: 1 Occupation: Farmer Groom's POB: Lee County,

Virginia Groom's father POB: Tennessee Groom's mother POB: Russell County, Virginia
Date of marriage: 4 September 1890
Bride: Sinda Stidham Residence: Leslie County, Kentucky Age: 39 Number of Marriages: 1 Bride's POB: Perry County, Kentucky Bride's father POB: Blank Bride's mother POB: Blank Marriage Book 7, page 387

Groom: William McKinney Residence: Leslie County, Kentucky Age: 23 Number of Marriages: Blank Occupation: Farmer Groom's POB: Clay County, Kentucky Groom's father POB: Lee County, Virginia Groom's mother POB: Lee County, Virginia
Date of marriage: 17 February 1887
Bride: Sarah Pace Residence: Leslie County, Kentucky Age: 17 Number of Marriages: Blank Bride's POB: Blank Bride's father POB: Blank Bride's mother POB: Blank Marriage Book 7, Page 125

Melton

Groom: Abner F. Melton Residence: Leslie County, Kentucky Age: 23 Number of Marriages: Blank Occupation: Farmer Groom's POB: Perry County, Kentucky Groom's father POB: Perry County, Kentucky Groom's mother POB: Harlan County, Kentucky
Date of marriage: 9 April 1889
Bride: Sarah Farler Residence: Perry County, Kentucky Age: 19 Number of Marriages: Blank Bride's POB: Perry County, Kentucky Bride's father POB: Perry County, Kentucky Bride's mother POB: Perry County, Kentucky Marriage Book 7, page 291

Groom: Russel Melton Residence: Leslie County, Kentucky Age: 24 Number of Marriages: Blank Occupation: Farmer Groom's POB: Perry County, Kentucky Groom's father POB: Blank Groom's mother POB: Blank
Date of marriage: 28 April 1886
Bride: Susan Messer Residence: Perry County, Kentucky Age: 22 Number of Marriages: 1 Bride's POB: Perry County, Kentucky Bride's father POB: Blank Bride's mother POB: Blank Marriage Book 7, page 61

Groom: William Melton Residence: Leslie County, Kentucky Age: 21 Number of Marriages: Blank Occupation: Farmer Groom's POB: Perry County, Kentucky Groom's father POB: Perry County, Kentucky Groom's mother POB: Wise County, Virginia
Date of marriage: 5 February 1891

Bride: Nancy Vanover Residence: Leslie County, Kentucky Age: 16
Number of Marriages: Blank Bride's POB: Perry County, Kentucky Bride's father POB: Russel County, Virginia Bride's mother POB: North Carolina
Remarks: The following note appears in the record: "February the 4th, 1891. To any clerk of Leslie County to give William Melton license to marry Nancy Vanover. Signed: Her mark "X" Patsy Vanover."
Marriage Book 7, page 417

Messer

Groom: Benjamin Messer Residence: Leslie County, Kentucky Age: 28
Number of Marriages: Blank Occupation: Farmer Groom's POB: Perry County, Kentucky Groom's father POB: Knox County, Kentucky Groom's mother POB: Perry County, Kentucky
Date of marriage: 8 August 1889
Bride: Rachel Melton Residence: Leslie County, Kentucky Age: 16 Number of Marriages: Blank Bride's POB: Perry County, Kentucky Bride's father POB: Harlan County, Kentucky Bride's mother POB: Harlan County, Kentucky Marriage Book 7, page 303

Groom: Madison Messer Residence: Perry County. Kentucky Age: 22
Number of Marriages: Blank Occupation: Farmer Groom's POB: Perry County, Kentucky Groom's father POB: Perry County, Kentucky Groom's mother POB: Perry County, Kentucky
Date of marriage: 15 July 1886
Bride: Elizabeth Melton Residence: Leslie County, Kentucky Age: 16
Number of Marriages: Blank Bride's POB: Perry County, Kentucky Bride's father POB: Perry County, Kentucky Bride's mother POB: Harlan County, Kentucky Marriage Book 7, page 81

Miller

Groom: George W. Miller Residence: Big Creek, Kentucky Age: 25
Number of Marriages: 2 Occupation: Farmer Groom's POB: Blank Groom's father POB: Blank Groom's mother POB: Blank
Date of marriage: 4 May 1892
Bride: Sallie Sisemore Residence: Big Creek, Kentucky Age: 22 Number of Marriages: 2 Bride's POB: Blank Bride's father POB: Blank Bride's mother POB: Blank
Remarks: Married at Jesse Couch's residence in Leslie County, Kentucky.
Marriage Book 7, page 487

Miniard

Groom: Joseph Miniard Residence: Perry County, Kentucky Age: 27
Number of Marriages: Blank Occupation: Farmer Groom's POB: Harlan
County, Kentucky Groom's father POB: Harlan County, Kentucky Groom's
mother POB: Perry County, Kentucky
Date of marriage: 12 February 1890
Bride: Rutha Jane Maggard Residence: Leslie County, Kentucky Age: 20
Number of Marriages: Blank Bride's POB: Perry County, Kentucky Bride's
father POB: Perry County, Kentucky Bride's mother POB: Harlan County,
Kentucky Marriage Book 7, page 349

Morgan

Groom: A. B. Morgan Residence: Hyden, Kentucky Age: 21 Number of
Marriages: Blank Occupation: Farmer Groom's POB: Clay County,
Kentucky Groom's father POB: Perry County, Kentucky Groom's mother
POB: Clay County, Kentucky
Date of marriage: 5 October 1893
Bride: Mary Mattingly Residence: Hyden, Kentucky Age: 18 Number of
Marriages: Blank Bride's POB: Clay County, Kentucky Bride's father POB:
Clay County, Kentucky Bride's mother POB: Clay County, Kentucky
Remarks: The following note appears in the record: To the Clerk of the
County Court. This is your authorization to issue marriage license for A. B.
Morgan and Mary Sally Mattingly. Signed: J. Mattingly Signed: M. J.
Mattingly."
Marriage Book 7, page 567

Groom: G. M. Morgan Residence: Leslie County, Kentucky Age: 22
Number of Marriages: Blank Occupation: School teacher Groom's POB:
Perry County, Kentucky Groom's father POB: Perry County, Kentucky
Groom's mother POB: Perry County, Kentucky
Date of marriage: 24 June 1893
Bride: Martha Helton Residence: Leslie County, Kentucky Age: 16 Number
of Marriages: Blank Bride's POB: Perry County, Kentucky Bride's father
POB: Perry County, Kentucky Bride's mother POB: Perry County,
Kentucky Marriage Book 7, page 559

Groom: G. W. Morgan Residence: Leslie County, Kentucky Age: 30
Number of Marriages: Blank Occupation: Merchant Groom's POB: Perry
County, Kentucky Groom's father POB: Blank Groom's mother POB:
Blank
Date of marriage: 22 November 1891
Bride: Orleana Combs Residence: Leslie County, Kentucky Age: 22
Number of Marriages: Blank Bride's POB: Perry County, Kentucky Bride's
father POB: Blank Bride's mother POB: Blank Marriage Book 7, page 455

Groom: Garland Morgan Residence: Short Creek, Leslie County, Kentucky Age: 21 Number of Marriages: 1 Occupation: Farmer Groom's POB: Leslie County, Kentucky Groom's father POB: Clay County, Kentucky Groom's mother POB: Clay County, Kentucky
Date of marriage: 14 April 1894
Bride: Mary Begley Residence: Hyden, Kentucky Age: 18 Number of Marriages: 1 Bride's POB: Clay County, Kentucky Bride's father POB: Owsley County, Kentucky Bride's mother POB: Clay County, Kentucky
Remarks: Married at A. B. Dixon's home.
Marriage Book 7, page 599

Groom: Hughes Morgan Residence: Leslie County, Kentucky Age: 33 Number of Marriages: 1 Occupation: Farmer Groom's POB: Blank Groom's father POB: Blank Groom's mother POB: Blank
Date of marriage: 8 February 1889
Bride: Peggy Howard Residence: Leslie County, Kentucky Age: 48 Number of Marriages: Blank Bride's POB: Harlan County, Kentucky Bride's father POB: Harlan County, Kentucky Bride's mother POB: Harlan County, Kentucky Marriage Book 7, page 267

Groom: Ira Morgan Residence: Leslie County, Kentucky Age: 25 Number of Marriages: Blank Occupation: Farmer and school teacher Groom's POB: Perry County, Kentucky Groom's father POB: Perry County, Kentucky Groom's mother POB: Perry County, Kentucky
Date of marriage: 12 December 1893
Bride: Jane Morgan Residence: Leslie County, Kentucky Age: 16 Number of Marriages: Blank Bride's POB: Perry County, Kentucky Bride's father POB: Perry County, Kentucky Bride's mother POB: Perry County, Kentucky
Remarks: The following note appears in the record: "Mr. J. M. Howard. Sir, Your are permitted to give marriage license to David Turner and Susan E. Baker. This the 7th day of October 1893. Signed: L. G. Baker."
Marriage Book 7, page 575

Groom: James Morgan Residence: Leslie County, Kentucky Age: 27 Number of Marriages: Blank Occupation: Merchant Groom's POB: Clay County, Kentucky Groom's father POB: Blank Groom's mother POB: Blank
Date of marriage: 8 October 1890
Bride: Prelia Metcalf Residence: Harlan County, Kentucky Age: 22 Number of Marriages: Blank Bride's POB: Harlan County, Kentucky Bride's father POB: Blank Bride's mother POB: Blank Marriage Book 7, page 401

Groom: John E. Morgan Residence: Leslie County, Kentucky Age: 26
Number of Marriages: Blank Occupation: Farmer Groom's POB: Perry
County, Kentucky Groom's father POB: Clay County, Kentucky Groom's
mother POB: Clay County, Kentucky
Date of marriage: 13 January 1886
Bride: Alice Napier Residence: Leslie County, Kentucky Age: 18 Number
of Marriages: Blank Bride's POB: Clay County, Kentucky Bride's father
POB: Clay County, Kentucky Bride's mother POB: Clay County, Kentucky
Marriage Book 7, Page 33

Groom: Taylor Morgan Residence: Hyden, Kentucky Age: 27 Number of
Marriages: 2 Occupation: Blank Groom's POB: Clay County, Kentucky
Groom's father POB: Harlan County, Kentucky Groom's mother POB: Clay
County, Kentucky
Date of marriage: 6 May 1894
Bride: Ella J. Howard Residence: Hyden, Kentucky Age: 17 Number of
Marriages: 1 Bride's POB: Blank Bride's father POB: Harlan County,
Kentucky Bride's mother POB: Harlan County, Kentucky
Remarks: Married at J. M. Howard's home.
Marriage Book 7, page 603

Groom: Thomas Morgan Residence: Leslie County, Kentucky Age: 23
Number of Marriages: Blank Occupation: Farmer Groom's POB: Clay
County, Kentucky Groom's father POB: Harlan County, Kentucky Groom's
mother POB: Clay County, Kentucky
Date of marriage: 18 March 1887
Bride: Molly Napier Residence: Leslie County, Kentucky Age: 17
Number of Marriages: Blank Bride's POB: Clay County, Kentucky Bride's
father POB: Harlan County, Kentucky Bride's mother POB: Clay County,
Kentucky Marriage Book 7, Page 133

Morris

Groom: G. O. Morris Residence: Perry County, Kentucky Age: 25 Number
of Marriages: 1 Occupation: Farmer Groom's POB: Perry County, Kentucky
Groom's father POB: North Carolina Groom's mother POB: Perry County,
Kentucky
Date of marriage: 20 January 1886
Bride: Jane Stidham Residence: Leslie County, Kentucky Age: 21
Number of Marriages: Blank Bride's POB: Perry County, Kentucky Bride's
father POB: Blank Bride's mother POB: Blank Marriage Book 7, page 35

Mosley

Groom: Henderson Mosley Residence: Leslie County, Kentucky Age: 18 Number of Marriages: 1 Occupation: Farmer Groom's POB: Clay County, Kentucky Groom's father POB: Not known Groom's mother POB: Not known
Date of marriage: 22 September 1887
Bride: Susan Napier Residence: Leslie County, Kentucky Age: Not known Number of Marriages: 1 Bride's POB: Clay County, Kentucky Bride's father POB: Clay County, Kentucky Bride's mother POB: Clay County, Kentucky Marriage Book 7, Page 167

Mullins

Groom: W. J. Mullins Residence: Leslie County, Kentucky Age: 25 Number of Marriages: Blank Occupation: Carpenter and stone cutter Groom's POB: Laurel County, Kentucky Groom's father POB: Indiana Groom's mother POB: Laurel County, Kentucky
Date of marriage: 12 November 1891
Bride: Dosa Begley Residence: Leslie County, Kentucky Age: 18 Number of Marriages: Blank Bride's POB: Clay County, Kentucky Bride's father POB: Clay County, Kentucky Bride's mother POB: BlankMarriage Book 7, page 415

Muncy

Groom: Allen Muncy Residence: Leslie County, Kentucky Age: 21 Number of Marriages: Blank Occupation: Farmer Groom's POB: Clay County, Kentucky Groom's father POB: Clay County, Kentucky Groom's mother POB: Clay County, Kentucky
Date of marriage: 5 July 1890
Bride: Polly Wooton Residence: Leslie County, Kentucky Age: 16 Number of Marriages: Blank Bride's POB: Perry County, Kentucky Bride's father POB: Perry County, Kentucky Bride's mother POB: Perry County, Kentucky Marriage Book 7, page 373

Groom: Jasper Muncy Residence: Leslie County, Kentucky Age: 25 Number of Marriages: 1 Occupation: Farmer Groom's POB: Perry County, Kentucky Groom's father POB: Unknown Groom's mother POB: Harlan County, Kentucky
Date of marriage: 28 September 1888
Bride: Elizabeth Whitehead Residence: Leslie County, Kentucky Age: 31 Number of Marriages: 1 Bride's POB: Kentucky Bride's father POB: Blank Bride's mother POB: Blank

Remarks: Note appears in the record as follows: "The County Clerk of Leslie County. You will please grant Bijha Roberts marriage license. This the 4th day of October 1888. Signed: Otta Roberts."
Marriage Book 7, page 241

Groom: John Muncy Residence: Leslie County, Kentucky Age: About 34 Number of Marriages: Blank Occupation: Farmer Groom's POB: Clay County, Kentucky Groom's father POB: Blank Groom's mother POB: Blank
Date of marriage: 19 June 1886
Bride: Melda Sisemore Residence: Leslie County, Kentucky Age: 21 Number of Marriages: Blank Bride's POB: Clay County, Kentucky Bride's father POB: Blank Bride's mother POB: Blank Marriage Book 7, Page 75

Murrell

Groom: Grant Murrell Residence: Leslie County, Kentucky Age: 22 Number of Marriages: 1 Occupation: Farmer Groom's POB: Perry County, Kentucky Groom's father POB: Perry County, Kentucky Groom's mother POB: Perry County, Kentucky
Date of marriage: 9 December 1892
Bride: Nancy Bowling Residence: Perry County, Kentucky Age: 17 Number of Marriages: 1 Bride's POB: Perry County, Kentucky Bride's father POB: Perry County, Kentucky Bride's mother POB: Clay County, Kentucky
Remarks: The following note appears in the record: "Wooton Creek, Kentucky. June 15, 1892. This is to authorize any clerk of Leslie County Court to give marriage license for the rites of matrimony between my daughter, Rebecca Napier and M. B. Feltner. Signed: H. N. Napier. //To the count clerk of Leslie. I hereby authorize you to issue marriage license between Nancy Bowling and Grant Murrell. This December 3rd day of 1892. Signed: Jon E. Bowling. Signed Sally Bowling."
Marriage Book 7, page 525

Nance

Groom: William Nance Residence: Leslie County, Kentucky Age: 18 Number of Marriages: Blank Occupation: Farmer Groom's POB: Perry County, Kentucky Groom's father POB: Harlan County, Kentucky Groom's mother POB: Perry County, Kentucky
Date of marriage: 19 April 1888
Bride: Elizabeth Lewis Residence: Leslie County, Kentucky Age: 16 Number of Marriages: Blank Bride's POB: Perry County, Kentucky Bride's father POB: Perry County, Kentucky Bride's mother POB: North Carolina

Remarks: Note appears in the record as follows: "Mr. J. M. Howard. Sir, please let James Lewis have license for himself and Elizabeth Lewis, if he calls for them. They are both underage. This the 27th day of December 1887. Signed: His mark "X" James Lewis Signed: His mark "X" David Lewis
Marriage Book 7, page 219

Nantz

Groom: Daniel Nantz Residence: Leslie County, Kentucky Age: 18 Number of Marriages: Blank Occupation: Farmer Groom's POB: Harlan County, Kentucky Groom's father POB: Clay County, Kentucky Groom's mother POB: Clay County, Kentucky
Date of marriage: 16 July 1891
Bride: Rebecca Napier Residence: Leslie County, Kentucky Age: 19 Number of Marriages: Blank Bride's POB: Clay County, Kentucky Bride's father POB: Harlan County, Kentucky Bride's mother POB: Clay County, Kentucky
Remarks: The following note appears in the record: "This the 16th of July 1891. This is to certify that I authorize the County Clerk to issue marriage license for Dan Nantz. Signed: John Nantz. // This is to certify that I authorize the County Court Clerk to issue marriage license for Rebecca Napier. Signed: Kinyard Napier."
Marriage Book 7, page 433

Napier

Groom: A. B. Napier Residence: Leslie County, Kentucky Age: 34 Number of Marriages: 2 Occupation: Farmer Groom's POB: Clay County, Kentucky Groom's father POB: Harlan County, Kentucky Groom's mother POB: Clay County, Kentucky
Date of marriage: 22 August 1892
Bride: Lucy Sizemore Residence: Clay County, Kentucky Age: 21 Number of Marriages: 2 Bride's POB: Clay County, Kentucky Bride's father POB: Clay County, Kentucky Bride's mother POB: North Carolina
Remarks: The following note appears in the record: "Dear Sir. I authorize you to issue marriage license for Judy Shepherd to marry W. H. Flanery. This October 7, 1892. Signed: Elisha Shepherd."
Marriage Book 7, page 507

Groom: Adrian Napier Residence: Leslie County, Kentucky Age: Blank Number of Marriages: 1 Occupation: Farmer Groom's POB: Blank Groom's father POB: Blank Groom's mother POB: Blank
Date of marriage: 3 March 1886

Bride: Sarah Couch Residence: Leslie County, Kentucky Age: 30 Number of Marriages: 2 Bride's POB: Clay County, Kentucky Bride's father POB: Blank Bride's mother POB: Blank Marriage Book 7, page 49

Groom: Ballard Napier Residence: Leslie County, Kentucky Age: 17 Number of Marriages: 1 Occupation: Farmer Groom's POB: Clay County, Kentucky Groom's father POB: Clay County, Kentucky Groom's mother POB: Clay County, Kentucky
Date of marriage: 1 August 1890
Bride: Polly Johnson Residence: Leslie County, Kentucky Age: 16 Number of Marriages: 1 Bride's POB: Clay County, Kentucky Bride's father POB: Clay County, Kentucky Bride's mother POB: Clay County, Kentucky
Remarks: The following note appears in the record: "A few lines from Thomas Johnson and wife to the Clerk of Leslie County to give marriage license for Ballard Napier and Polly Johnson and it will be all right with me. Signed: Thomas Johnson and witness this July 30, 1890."
Marriage Book 7, page 379

Groom: Dillion Napier Residence: Clay County, Kentucky Age: 20 Number of Marriages: Blank Occupation: Farmer Groom's POB: Clay County, Kentucky Groom's father POB: Clay County, Kentucky Groom's mother POB: Clay County, Kentucky
Date of marriage: 15 April 1890
Bride: Ellen Sisemore Residence: Clay County, Kentucky Age: 16 Number of Marriages: Blank Bride's POB: Clay County, Kentucky Bride's father POB: Blank Bride's mother POB: Blank
Remarks: The following note appears in the record: "This is authorized by Miss Jane Sisemore and John Hampton Napier that Leslie County Court Clerk or deputy should give license to Miss Ellen Sisemore and Dillion Napier. This April 14, 1890."
Marriage Book 7, page 363

Groom: Henry Napier Residence: Leslie County, Kentucky Age: 27 Number of Marriages: 1 Occupation: Farmer Groom's POB: Clay County, Kentucky Groom's father POB: Clay County, Kentucky Groom's mother POB: Clay County, Kentucky
Date of marriage: 18 August 1890
Bride: May Sisemore Residence: Leslie County, Kentucky Age: 29 Number of Marriages: Blank Bride's POB: Clay County, Kentucky Bride's father POB: Blank Bride's mother POB: Blank Marriage Book 7, page 383

Groom: Jackson Napier Residence: Leslie County, Kentucky Age: 23 Number of Marriages: Blank Occupation: Farmer Groom's POB: Clay

County, Kentucky Groom's father POB: Clay County, Kentucky Groom's mother POB: Clay County, Kentucky
Date of marriage: 21 July 1891
Bride: Martha Couch Residence: Leslie County, Kentucky Age: 18 Number of Marriages: Blank Bride's POB: Clay County, Kentucky Bride's father POB: Clay County, Kentucky Bride's mother POB: Clay County, Kentucky
Remarks: The following note appears in the record: "July the 21, 1891. Mr. J. M. Howard. I authorize you to give Jack Napier license to marry my girl. Signed: Cole Couch."
Marriage Book 7, page 435

Groom: John Napier Residence: Leslie County, Kentucky Age: 22 Number of Marriages: 1 Occupation: Farmer Groom's POB: Clay County, Kentucky Groom's father POB: Blank Groom's mother POB: Clay County, Kentucky
Date of marriage: 20 January 1888
Bride: Rebecca Morris Residence: Leslie County, Kentucky Age: 23 Number of Marriages: Blank Bride's POB: Blank Bride's father POB: Blank Bride's mother POB: Blank Marriage Book 7, page 197

Groom: Lincoln Napier Residence: Leslie County, Kentucky Age: 26 Number of Marriages: Blank Occupation: Farmer Groom's POB: Clay County, Kentucky Groom's father POB: Harlan County, Kentucky Groom's mother POB: Clay County, Kentucky
Date of marriage: 6 August 1888
Bride: Martha Asher Residence: Leslie County, Kentucky Age: 20 Number of Marriages: Blank Bride's POB: Clay County, Kentucky Bride's father POB: Clay County, Kentucky Bride's mother POB: Clay County, Kentucky
Marriage Book 7, page 233

Groom: Mc Napier Residence: Leslie County, Kentucky Age: 20 Number of Marriages: Blank Occupation: Farmer Groom's POB: Clay County, Kentucky Groom's father POB: Harlan County, Kentucky Groom's mother POB: Clay County, Kentucky
Date of marriage: 26 May 1887
Bride: Semmie Sisemore Residence: Leslie County, Kentucky Age: 20 Number of Marriages: Blank Bride's POB: Clay County, Kentucky Bride's father POB: Clay County, Kentucky Bride's mother POB: Breathitt County, Kentucky Marriage Book 7, Page 147

Groom: William Napier Residence: Leslie County, Kentucky Age: 28 Number of Marriages: Blank Occupation: Farmer Groom's POB: Clay County, Kentucky Groom's father POB: Harlan County, Kentucky Groom's mother POB: Clay County, Kentucky
Date of marriage: 31 August 1889

Bride: Hannah Nance Residence: Leslie County, Kentucky Age: 17 Number of Marriages: Blank Bride's POB: Blank Bride's father POB: Blank Bride's mother POB: Blank Marriage Book 7, page 307

North

Groom: Wilson North Residence: Leslie County, Kentucky Age: 18 Number of Marriages: Blank Occupation: Farmer Groom's POB: Clay County, Kentucky Groom's father POB: Clay County, Kentucky Groom's mother POB: Harlan County, Kentucky
Date of marriage: 20 September 1890
Bride: Gelanie Wilson Residence: Leslie County, Kentucky Age: 18 Number of Marriages: 1 Bride's POB: Clay County, Kentucky Bride's father POB: Harlan County, Kentucky Bride's mother POB: Harlan County, Kentucky Marriage Book 7, page 393

Oliver

Groom: James Oliver Residence: Perry County, Kentucky Age: 22 Number of Marriages: Blank Occupation: Farmer Groom's POB: Perry County, Kentucky Groom's father POB: Blank Groom's mother POB: Clay County, Kentucky
Date of marriage: 24 December 1888
Bride: Alice Howard Residence: Leslie County, Kentucky Age: 19 Number of Marriages: Blank Bride's POB: Clay County, Kentucky Bride's father POB: Blank Bride's mother POB: Blank
Remarks: Note in the record reads as follows: "December 20th, 1888. Mr. Mat Howard. Sir, Please give license to James Oliver and Alice Howard. Signed: Gilbert Howard // Mr. Clerk. Please let Jackson Duff have license to marry Silvania Burkhart and oblige me this the 23 of October 1886. Signed: S. C. Burkhart."
Marriage Book 7, page 259

Groom: Sherman Oliver Residence: Perry County, Kentucky Age: 21 Number of Marriages: 1 Occupation: Farmer Groom's POB: Perry County, Kentucky Groom's father POB: Perry County, Kentucky Groom's mother POB: Clay County, Kentucky
Date of marriage: 16 August 1894
Bride: Nancy Parker Residence: Leslie County, Kentucky Age: 15 Number of Marriages: 1 Bride's POB: Leslie County, Kentucky Bride's father POB: Knox County, Kentucky Bride's mother POB: Clay County, Kentucky
Remarks: Married at the home of Franklin Parker.
Marriage Book 7, page 625

Pace

Groom: William Pace Residence: Leslie County, Kentucky Age: 28 Number of Marriages: Blank Occupation: Farmer Groom's POB: Harlan County, Kentucky Groom's father POB: Harlan County, Kentucky Groom's mother POB: North Carolina
Date of marriage: 24 July 1888
Bride: Nancy Morgan Residence: Leslie County, Kentucky Age: 23 Number of Marriages: 1 Bride's POB: Harlan County, Kentucky Bride's father POB: Blank Bride's mother POB: Harlan County, Kentucky Marriage Book 7, Page 231

Parker

Groom: Elijah Parker Residence: Leslie County, Kentucky Age: 17 Number of Marriages: Blank Occupation: Farmer Groom's POB: Clay County, Kentucky Groom's father POB: Knox County, Kentucky Groom's mother POB: Clay County, Kentucky
Date of marriage: 23 July 1894
Bride: Sally Ann Collins Residence: Leslie County, Kentucky Age: 17 Number of Marriages: Blank Bride's POB: Clay County, Kentucky Bride's father POB: Blank Bride's mother POB: Blank Marriage Book 7, page 621

Parks

Groom: Hiram Parks Residence: Cutshin, Kentucky Age: 19 Number of Marriages: 1 Occupation: Farmer Groom's POB: Clay County, Kentucky Groom's father POB: Perry County, Kentucky Groom's mother POB: Virginia
Date of marriage: 8 June 1893
Bride: Betty Ann Wells Residence: Leslie County, Kentucky Age: 15 Number of Marriages: 1 Bride's POB: Leslie County, Kentucky Bride's father POB: Perry County, Kentucky Bride's mother POB: Perry County, Kentucky
Remarks: Married at Bride's Mother's residence. The following note appears in the record: "This June 4, 1893. I certify that she is her own agent. Signed Rebecca Cornett Signed Berry Ann Wells. // August 24, 1893. Mr. J. M. Howard. Sir, you will please issue marriage license for my daughter, Rebecca and Willis McCollum, as it is my request by doing so you will oblige me. Signed His mark "X" Hamp Napier."
Marriage Book 7, page 553

Groom: William Parks Residence: Leslie County, Kentucky Age: 21 Number of Marriages: Blank Occupation: Farmer Groom's POB: Clay

County, Kentucky Groom's father POB: Clay County, Kentucky Groom's mother POB: Virginia
Date of marriage: 23 January 1891
Bride: Rebecca Stidham Residence: Leslie County, Kentucky Age: 16 Number of Marriages: Blank Bride's POB: Perry County, Kentucky Bride's father POB: Blank Bride's mother POB: Perry County, Kentucky Marriage Book 7, page 413

Pennington

Groom: Alex Pennington Residence: Blank Age: 29 Number of Marriages: Blank Occupation: Farmer Groom's POB: Harlan County, Kentucky Groom's father POB: Harlan County, Kentucky Groom's mother POB: Harlan County, Kentucky
Date of marriage: No date (Most likely 1884)
Bride: Elizabeth Sergeant Residence: Harlan County, Kentucky Age: 22 Number of Marriages: Blank Bride's POB: Harlan County, Kentucky Bride's father POB: Harlan County, Kentucky Bride's mother POB: Harlan County, Kentucky Marriage Book 7, Page 3

Groom: James Pennington Residence: Leslie County, Kentucky Age: 50 Number of Marriages: 1 Occupation: Farmer Groom's POB: Blank Groom's father POB: Blank Groom's mother POB: Blank
Date of marriage: 21 April 1886
Bride: Polly Eastridge Residence: Leslie County, Kentucky Age: 35 Number of Marriages: Blank Bride's POB: Blank Bride's father POB: Blank Bride's mother POB: Blank Marriage Book 7, page 57

Groom: Johnathan Pennington Residence: Leslie County, Kentucky Age: 19 Number of Marriages: Blank Occupation: Farmer Groom's POB: Perry County, Kentucky Groom's father POB: Harlan County, Kentucky Groom's mother POB: Harlan County, Kentucky
Date of marriage: 20 November 1886
Bride: Mary Muncy Residence: Leslie County, Kentucky Age: 21 Number of Marriages: Blank Bride's POB: Harlan County, Kentucky Bride's father POB: Blank Bride's mother POB: Blank
Remarks: Note in the record reads as follows: "To the Clerk of Leslie County. This is to certify that I am willing for you to issue marriage license to my son Johnathan Pennington and Mary Muncy. This November 18, 1886. Signed William Pennington."
Marriage Book 7, Page 113

Groom: William Pennington Residence: Leslie County, Kentucky Age: 19 Number of Marriages: Blank Occupation: Farmer Groom's POB: Perry

County, Kentucky Groom's father POB: Perry County, Kentucky Groom's mother POB: Perry County, Kentucky
Date of marriage: 27 August 1887
Bride: Polly Howard Residence: Leslie County, Kentucky Age: 18 Number of Marriages: Blank Bride's POB: Perry County, Kentucky Bride's father POB: Harlan County, Kentucky Bride's mother POB: Blank Marriage Book 7, Page 163

Groom: William Pennington Residence: Leslie County, Kentucky Age: 35 Number of Marriages: Blank Occupation: Farmer Groom's POB: Harlan County, Kentucky Groom's father POB: Harlan County, Kentucky Groom's mother POB: Harlan County, Kentucky
Date of marriage: 29 October 1894
Bride: Sarah Noe Residence: Leslie County, Kentucky Age: 34 Number of Marriages: Blank Bride's POB: Blank Bride's father POB: Blank Bride's mother POB: Blank Marriage Book 7, page 637

Rice

Groom: Frank Rice Residence: Leslie County, Kentucky Age: 19 Number of Marriages: Blank Occupation: Farmer Groom's POB: Clay County, Kentucky Groom's father POB: Letcher County, Kentucky Groom's mother POB: Clay County, Kentucky
Date of marriage: 29 December 1885
Bride: Elizabeth Johnson Residence: Leslie County, Kentucky Age: 19 Number of Marriages: Blank Bride's POB: Perry County, Kentucky Bride's father POB: Blank Bride's mother POB: Blank Marriage Book 7, page 31

Groom: Henry Rice Residence: Perry County, Kentucky Age: 18 Number of Marriages: 1 Occupation: Farmer Groom's POB: Perry County, Kentucky Groom's father POB: Perry County, Kentucky Groom's mother POB: Perry County, Kentucky
Date of marriage: 27 November 1888
Bride: Sally Estep Residence: Leslie County, Kentucky Age: 21 Number of Marriages: Blank Bride's POB: Perry County, Kentucky Bride's father POB: Perry County, Kentucky Bride's mother POB: Perry County, Kentucky Marriage Book 7, page 251

Roark

Groom: Hance Roark Residence: Leslie County, Kentucky Age: 26 Number of Marriages: Blank Occupation: Farmer Groom's POB: Clay County, Kentucky Groom's father POB: Clay County, Kentucky Groom's mother POB: Blank Date of marriage: Clay County, Kentucky

Bride: 1 May 1889
Residence: Sabra Sisemore Age: 18 Number of Marriages: Blank Bride's POB: Clay County, Kentucky Bride's father POB: Clay County, Kentucky Bride's mother POB: Clay County, Kentucky
Remarks: Note appears in the records as follows: "April the 24th, 1889. Mr. Mattison Howard. You will give Henderson Roark marriage license by our consent. Signed: Robert Sisemore. Signed: Her mark "X" Mahaly Sisemore
Marriage Book 7, page 293

Roberts

Groom: Abijah Roberts Residence: Leslie County, Kentucky Age: 19 Number of Marriages: Blank Occupation: Farmer Groom's POB: Clay County, Kentucky Groom's father POB: Clay County, Kentucky Groom's mother POB: Clay County, Kentucky
Date of marriage: 3 October 1888
Bride: Susan Roberts Residence: Leslie County, Kentucky Age: 19 Number of Marriages: Blank Bride's POB: Perry County, Kentucky Bride's father POB: Clay County, Kentucky Bride's mother POB: Perry County, Kentucky
Marriage Book 7, page 243

Groom: Anderson Roberts Residence: Blank Age: Blank Number of Marriages: Blank Occupation: Blank Groom's POB: Blank Groom's father POB: Blank Groom's mother POB: Blank
Date of marriage: 1 December 1891
Bride: Elizabeth Griffitts Residence: Blank Age: Blank Number of Marriages: Blank Bride's POB: Blank Bride's father POB: Blank Bride's mother POB: Blank
Remarks: Marriage bond was completed along with marriage certificate.
Marriage Book 7, page 477

Groom: Felix Roberts Residence: Blank Age: Blank Number of Marriages: Blank Occupation: Blank Groom's POB: Blank Groom's father POB: Blank Groom's mother POB: Blank
Date of marriage: 30 July 1892
Bride: Martha Gibson Residence: Blank Age: Blank Number of Marriages: Blank Bride's POB: Blank Bride's father POB: Blank Bride's mother POB: Blank
Remarks: Marriage bond was completed.
Marriage Book 7, page 499

Groom: Frank Roberts Residence: Leslie County, Kentucky Age: 19 Number of Marriages: Blank Occupation: Farmer Groom's POB: Clay

County, Kentucky Groom's father POB: Clay County, Kentucky Groom's mother POB: Clay County, Kentucky
Date of marriage: 21 March 1889
Bride: Polly Gay Residence: Leslie County, Kentucky Age: 16 Number of Marriages: Blank Bride's POB: Clay County, Kentucky Bride's father POB: Clay County, Kentucky Bride's mother POB: Clay County, Kentucky
Marriage Book 7, page 281

Groom: James A. Roberts Residence: Leslie County, Kentucky Age: Blank Number of Marriages: Blank Occupation: Carpenter Groom's POB: Wise County, Virginia Groom's father POB: Lee County, Virginia Groom's mother POB: Lee County, Virginia
Date of marriage: 11 October 1886
Bride: Nancy Pace Residence: Leslie County, Kentucky Age: 28 Number of Marriages: 2 Bride's POB: Perry County, Kentucky Bride's father POB: Perry County, Kentucky Bride's mother POB: Harlan County, Kentucky Remarks: Note in the record reads as follows: " October 11th, 1886. Mr. County Court Clerk. I authorized Delaney Barger to license my Nancy the around framing for James Roberts and Nancy Pace. Signed A. B. Morgan."
Marriage Book 7, Page 109

Groom: M. C. Roberts Residence: Leslie County, Kentucky Age: 19 Number of Marriages: Blank Occupation: Farmer Groom's POB: Blank Groom's father POB: Blank Groom's mother POB: Blank
Date of marriage: 20 February 1886
Bride: Anna Maggard Residence: Leslie County, Kentucky Age: 19 Number of Marriages: Blank Bride's POB: Blank Bride's father POB: Blank Bride's mother POB: Blank Marriage Book 7, Page 43

Groom: Price Roberts Residence: Leslie County, Kentucky Age: 32 Number of Marriages: Blank Occupation: Farmer Groom's POB: Perry County, Kentucky Groom's father POB: Clay County, Kentucky Groom's mother POB: Clay County, Kentucky
Date of marriage: 25 February 1886
Bride: Vinie Collins Residence: Leslie County, Kentucky Age: 21 Number of Marriages: Blank Bride's POB: Clay County, Kentucky Bride's father POB: Blank Bride's mother POB: Blank Marriage Book 7, Page 47

Runals

Groom: Marinda Runals Residence: Leslie County, Kentucky Age: 24 Number of Marriages: Blank Occupation: Farmer Groom's POB: Owsley County, Kentucky Groom's father POB: Owsley County, Kentucky Groom's mother POB: Owsley County, Kentucky

Date of marriage: 20 August 1889
Bride: Elizabeth Bailey Residence: Leslie County, Kentucky Age: 18
Number of Marriages: Blank Bride's POB: Perry County, Kentucky Bride's father POB: Virginia Bride's mother POB: Perry County, Kentucky
Marriage Book 7, page 305

Sandlin

Groom: Carlo Sandlin Residence: Owsley County, Kentucky Age: 22
Number of Marriages: Blank Occupation: Farmer Groom's POB: Breathitt County, Kentucky Groom's father POB: Breathitt County, Kentucky Groom's mother POB: Owsley County, Kentucky
Date of marriage: 11 January 1888
Bride: Cordillie Jones Residence: Leslie County, Kentucky Age: 17
Number of Marriages: Blank Bride's POB: Clay County, Kentucky Bride's father POB: Blank Bride's mother POB: Blank Marriage Book 7, Page 195

Groom: Estill Sandlin Residence: Blank Age: Blank Number of Marriages: Blank Occupation: Blank Groom's POB: Blank Groom's father POB: Blank Groom's mother POB: Blank
Date of marriage: 20 June 1892
Bride: Elizabeth Bowling Residence: Blank Age: Blank Number of Marriages: Blank Bride's POB: Blank Bride's father POB: Blank Bride's mother POB: Blank
Remarks: Marriage bond completed. The following note appears in the record: "June 19, 1892. To the Clerk of Leslie County. You are permitted to issue marriage license for Elizabeth Bowling. Signed: Jesse B. Bowling."
Marriage Book 7, page 497

Scalf

Groom: David Scalf Residence: Clay County, Kentucky Age: 18 Number of Marriages: Blank Occupation: Farmer Groom's POB: Clay County, Kentucky Groom's father POB: Blank Groom's mother POB: Clay County, Kentucky
Date of marriage: 3 April 1893
Bride: Adaline Sizemore Residence: Leslie County, Kentucky Age: 22
Number of Marriages: Blank Bride's POB: Clay County, Kentucky Bride's father POB: Blank Bride's mother POB: Blank Marriage Book 7, page 547

Groom: Dillion Scalf Residence: Leslie County, Kentucky Age: 18
Number of Marriages: Blank Occupation: Farmer Groom's POB: Clay County, Kentucky Groom's father POB: Blank Groom's mother POB: Blank

Date of marriage: 18 December 1886
Bride: Killy Sisemore Residence: Leslie County, Kentucky Age: 22
Number of Marriages: Blank Bride's POB: Clay County, Kentucky Bride's father POB: Clay County, Kentucky Bride's mother POB: Clay County, Kentucky
Remarks: Note in the record reads as follows: "Please Mr. Madison Howard let Dillion Scalf have his license form under my hand. Signed Jesse Scalf."
Marriage Book 7, page 115

Groom: James Scalf Residence: Leslie County, Kentucky Age: 23 Number of Marriages: 1 Occupation: Farmer Groom's POB: Clay County, Kentucky Groom's father POB: Virginia Groom's mother POB: Clay County, Kentucky
Date of marriage: 12 July 1886
Bride: India Sisemore Residence: Leslie County, Kentucky Age: 25
Number of Marriages: Blank Bride's POB: Clay County, Kentucky Bride's father POB: Clay County, Kentucky Bride's mother POB: Clay County, Kentucky Marriage Book 7, Page 79

Shepherd

Groom: Elihu Shepherd Residence: Leslie County, Kentucky Age: 25 Number of Marriages: Blank Occupation: Farmer Groom's POB: Perry County, Kentucky Groom's father POB: Virginia Groom's mother POB: Virginia
Date of marriage: 20 April 1885
Bride: Eliza Jane Shepherd Residence: Leslie County, Kentucky Age: 17
Number of Marriages: Blank Bride's POB: Perry County, Kentucky Bride's father POB: Virginia Bride's mother POB: Letcher County, Kentucky
Remarks: There is a note in the marriage book on the Officer Stationary of J. M. Howard, Clerk of Leslie County, Kentucky dated June 11, 1892 as follows "Clerk of Leslie County Court, you are authorized to issue a marriage license for my daughter. Signed: A. J. Vanover.
Marriage Book 7, page 9

Groom: William Shepherd Residence: Wooton Creek, Kentucky Age: 19
Number of Marriages: 1 Occupation: Labor Groom's POB: Perry County, Kentucky Groom's father POB: Blank Groom's mother POB: Blank
Date of marriage: 11 June 1892
Bride: Dora Vanover Residence: Wooton Creek, Kentucky Age: 14 Number of Marriages: 1 Bride's POB: Perry County, Kentucky Bride's father POB: Perry County, Kentucky Bride's mother POB: Perry County, Kentucky

Remarks: The following note appears in the record: "This June 8, 1892. I give William Collins the authority to get license to marry my daughter, Lucindy Collins. Signed: Robert Collins."
Marriage Book 7, page 493

Simpson

Groom: Gabreal Simpson Residence: Leslie County, Kentucky Age: 33
Number of Marriages: 1 Occupation: Farmer Groom's POB: Blank Groom's father POB: Blank Groom's mother POB: Blank
Date of marriage: 20 April 1888
Bride: Lucy McDaniel Residence: Leslie County, Kentucky Age: Blank
Number of Marriages: Blank Bride's POB: Harlan County, Kentucky
Bride's father POB: Blank Bride's mother POB: Blank Marriage Book 7, page 223

Sisemore

Groom: Henry Sisemore Residence: Leslie County, Kentucky Age: 22
Number of Marriages: 1 Occupation: Farmer Groom's POB: Clay County, Kentucky Groom's father POB: Clay County, Kentucky Groom's mother POB: Clay County, Kentucky
Date of marriage: 15 march 1888
Bride: Betty Ann Baker Residence: Leslie County, Kentucky Age: 20
Number of Marriages: 1 Bride's POB: Blank Bride's father POB: Blank Bride's mother POB: Blank
Remarks: Note appears in the record as follows: "Mr. J. M. Howard. Please give Henry Sizemore and Betty Ann Baker license and oblige. Yours truly, L. G. Baker. Sworn before me by Henry Sisemore this March 15th, 1888. Signed E. C. G. Howard, Deputy Clerk of Leslie County Court."
Marriage Book 7, Page 213

Groom: Hiram Sisemore Residence: Leslie County, Kentucky Age: 24
Number of Marriages: Blank Occupation: Farmer Groom's POB: Clay County, Kentucky Groom's father POB: Clay County, Kentucky Groom's mother POB: Clay County, Kentucky
Date of marriage: 25 August 1886
Bride: Emiline Sisemore Residence: Leslie County, Kentucky Age: 15
Number of Marriages: Blank Bride's POB: Clay County, Kentucky Bride's father POB: Clay County, Kentucky Bride's mother POB: Clay County, Kentucky Marriage Book 7, page 95

Groom: Hiram Sisemore Residence: Leslie County, Kentucky Age: 25
Number of Marriages: Blank Occupation: Farmer Groom's POB: Clay

County, Kentucky Groom's father POB: Clay County, Kentucky Groom's mother POB: Floyd County, Kentucky
Date of marriage: 30 April 1891
Bride: Jane Roberts Residence: Leslie County, Kentucky Age: 19 Number of Marriages: Blank Bride's POB: Clay County, Kentucky Bride's father POB: Clay County, Kentucky Bride's mother POB: Clay County, Kentucky
Remarks: The following note appears in the record: "This the 29th day of April 1891. Mr. J. M. Howard. With my consent Jane Roberts is nineteen years old. Signed: Dan Howard."
Marriage Book 7, page 425

Groom: Ira Sisemore Residence: Leslie County, Kentucky Age: 19 Number of Marriages: Blank Occupation: Farmer Groom's POB: Clay County, Kentucky Groom's father POB: Blank Groom's mother POB: Blank
Date of marriage: 26 February 1894
Bride: Martha Napier Residence: Clay County, Kentucky Age: 17 Number of Marriages: Blank Bride's POB: Clay County, Kentucky Bride's father POB: Harlan County, Kentucky Bride's mother POB: Clay County, Kentucky Marriage Book 7, page 589

Groom: James Sisemore Residence: Leslie County, Kentucky Age: 24 Number of Marriages: Blank Occupation: Farmer Groom's POB: Clay County, Kentucky Groom's father POB: Clay County, Kentucky Groom's mother POB: Blank
Date of marriage: 23 July 1887
Bride: Malinda Lewis Residence: Leslie County, Kentucky Age: 17 Number of Marriages: Blank Bride's POB: Perry County, Kentucky Bride's father POB: Perry County, Kentucky Bride's mother POB: Perry County, Kentucky
Remarks: Note appears in the record as follows: " Mr. County Court Clerk. Sir, please give to James Sizemore and Malinda Lewis their marriage license. Signed: Jesse Lewis."
Marriage Book 7, Page 155

Groom: James Sisemore Residence: Hyden, Leslie County, Kentucky Age: 22 Number of Marriages: Blank Occupation: Farmer Groom's POB: Clay County, Kentucky Groom's father POB: Clay County, Kentucky Groom's mother POB: Clay County, Kentucky
Date of marriage: 1 February 1892
Bride: Emily Sisemore Residence: Leslie County, Kentucky Age: 19 Number of Marriages: Blank Bride's POB: Clay County, Kentucky Bride's father POB: Clay County, Kentucky Bride's mother POB: Clay County, Kentucky Marriage Book 7, page 481

Groom: Joseph Sisemore Residence: Hyden, Kentucky Age: 23 Number of Marriages: 1 Occupation: Blank Groom's POB: Clay County, Kentucky Groom's father POB: Blank Groom's mother POB: Blank
Date of marriage: 30 April 1892
Bride: Elizabeth Combs Residence: Hyden, Kentucky Age: 18 Number of Marriages: 1 Bride's POB: Perry County, Kentucky Bride's father POB: Perry County, Kentucky Bride's mother POB: Perry County, Kentucky
Remarks: Married at the G. W. Morgan residence in Hyden, Kentucky.
Marriage Book 7, page 485

Groom: Robert Sisemore Residence: Clay County, Kentucky Age: Blank Number of Marriages: 1 Occupation: Farmer Groom's POB: Clay County, Kentucky Groom's father POB: Clay County, Kentucky Groom's mother POB: Clay County, Kentucky
Date of marriage: 28 November 1888
Bride: Charity Woods Residence: Leslie County, Kentucky Age: 23 Number of Marriages: 1 Bride's POB: Clay County, Kentucky Bride's father POB: Clay County, Kentucky Bride's mother POB: Clay County, Kentucky
Marriage Book 7, page 255

Groom: William Sisemore Residence: Leslie County, Kentucky Age: 17 Number of Marriages: Blank Occupation: Farmer Groom's POB: Clay County, Kentucky Groom's father POB: Clay County, Kentucky Groom's mother POB: Clay County, Kentucky
Date of marriage: 16 June 1888
Bride: Joanah Sisemore Residence: Leslie County, Kentucky Age: 15 Number of Marriages: Blank Bride's POB: Perry County, Kentucky Bride's father POB: Perry County, Kentucky Bride's mother POB: Perry County, Kentucky
Remarks: Note in the record appears as follows: "December 8, 1887. Mr. J. M. Howard, Clerk of Court of Leslie. You are authorized to give James Lewis license to marry Mary Jane Howard. Respectfully yours. Signed: Jackson Howard. Signed: Martha Howard."
Marriage Book 7, page 229

Groom: William Sisemore Residence: Leslie County, Kentucky Age: 21 Number of Marriages: 1 Occupation: Farmer Groom's POB: Perry County, Kentucky Groom's father POB: Perry County, Kentucky Groom's mother POB: Perry County, Kentucky
Date of marriage: 20 March 1890
Bride: Sally Begley Residence: Leslie County, Kentucky Age: 16 Number of Marriages: Blank Bride's POB: Perry County, Kentucky Bride's father POB: Perry County, Kentucky Bride's mother POB: Perry County, Kentucky
Marriage Book 7, page 355

Sizemore

Groom: Luther Sizemore Residence: Leslie County, Kentucky Age: 21 Number of Marriages: 1 Occupation: Farmer Groom's POB: Clay County, Kentucky Groom's father POB: Clay County, Kentucky Groom's mother POB: Clay County, Kentucky
Date of marriage: 24 November 1892
Bride: Arra Napier Residence: Leslie County, Kentucky Age: 19 Number of Marriages: 1 Bride's POB: Blank Bride's father POB: Clay County, Kentucky Bride's mother POB: Blank
Remarks: The following note appears in the record: "November 9, 1892. Mr. J. M. Howard. Sir, You will please give Arra Napier a certificate for marring. Signed: J. N. Napier."
Marriage Book 7, page 523

Groom: William Sizemore Residence: Leslie County, Kentucky Age: 25 Number of Marriages: Blank Occupation: Farmer Groom's POB: Clay County, Kentucky Groom's father POB: Owsley County, Kentucky Groom's mother POB: Clay County, Kentucky
Date of marriage: 16 September 1893
Bride: Martha Nantz Residence: Leslie County, Kentucky Age: 18 Number of Marriages: Blank Bride's POB: Blank Bride's father POB: Blank Bride's mother POB: Blank Marriage Book 7, page 565

Skeens

Groom: Leander Skeens Residence: Leslie County, Kentucky Age: 23 Number of Marriages: Blank Occupation: Farmer Groom's POB: Perry County, Kentucky Groom's father POB: Not Known Groom's mother POB: Not Known
Date of marriage: 6 March 1890
Bride: July Ann Shepherd Residence: Leslie County, Kentucky Age: 17 Number of Marriages: Blank Bride's POB: Perry County, Kentucky Bride's father POB: Not Known Bride's mother POB: Not Known
Remarks: The following note appears in the record: "March 5th, 1890. This is to certify that I will give Leander Skeens let to get license to marry July Ann Shepherd. Signed: Clemon Shepherd."
Marriage Book 7, page 351

Smith

Groom: William Smith Residence: Leslie County, Kentucky Age: 19 Number of Marriages: Blank Occupation: Farmer Groom's POB: Clay

County, Kentucky Groom's father POB: Clay County, Kentucky Groom's mother POB: Blank
Date of marriage: 4 February 1889
Bride: Lucindia Asher Residence: Leslie County, Kentucky Age: 30 Number of Marriages: 1 Bride's POB: Blank Bride's father POB: Harlan County, Kentucky Bride's mother POB: Clay County, Kentucky
Remarks: Note appears in the record as follows: "The Clerk of Leslie County is hereby authorized to issue marriage license between my son William Smith and Lucindy Napier. Signed: J. Sara Smith Signed: Elijah Peters."
Marriage Book 7, page 265

Spurlock

Groom: David Spurlock Residence: Leslie County, Kentucky Age: 16 Number of Marriages: Blank Occupation: Farmer Groom's POB: Perry County, Kentucky Groom's father POB: Blank Groom's mother POB: Perry County, Kentucky
Date of marriage: 14 April 1888
Bride: Lucindia Gibson Residence: Leslie County, Kentucky Age: 17 Number of Marriages: Blank Bride's POB: Clay County, Kentucky Bride's father POB: Blank Bride's mother POB: Clay County, Kentucky
Remarks: Note appears in the record as follows: "April 12th, 1888. We the father Constance Gibson of Lucinda Calihan to give marriage license to her. Please Clerk from Sim Gibson // A few time from Jess Spurlock to Clerk of Leslie County, Kentucky to give marriage license between David Spurlock and Lucindy Calihan. This March the 13th day 1888.
Marriage Book 7, Page 217

Groom: John Spurlock Residence: Leslie County, Kentucky Age: 22 Number of Marriages: 1 Occupation: Farmer Groom's POB: Harlan County, Kentucky Groom's father POB: Harlan County, Kentucky Groom's mother POB: Harlan County, Kentucky
Date of marriage: 18 October 1892
Bride: Judia Lewis Residence: Leslie County, Kentucky Age: 16 Number of Marriages: 1 Bride's POB: Clay County, Kentucky Bride's father POB: Harlan County, Kentucky Bride's mother POB: Harlan County, Kentucky
Marriage Book 7, page 517

Stewart

Groom: William Stewart Residence: Leslie County, Kentucky Age: 53 Number of Marriages: 2 Occupation: Farmer Groom's POB: Laurel County,

Kentucky Groom's father POB: Virginia Groom's mother POB: Laurel County, Kentucky
Date of marriage: 23 June 1894
Bride: Mahala Saylor Residence: Leslie County, Kentucky Age: 38 Number of Marriages: 1 Bride's POB: Harlan County, Kentucky Bride's father POB: Blank Bride's mother POB: Blank Marriage Book 7, page 611

Stidham

Groom: Henderson Stidham Residence: Leslie County, Kentucky Age: 42 Number of Marriages: 2 Occupation: Farmer Groom's POB: Not known Groom's father POB: Not known Groom's mother POB: Not known
Date of marriage: 28 December 1887
Bride: Artha Sparks Residence: Leslie County, Kentucky Age: Not known Number of Marriages: 1 Bride's POB: Not known Bride's father POB: Not known Bride's mother POB: Not known Marriage Book 7, Page 187

Groom: Jackson Stidham Residence: Leslie County, Kentucky Age: 19 Number of Marriages: None Occupation: Farmer Groom's POB: Perry County, Kentucky Groom's father POB: Perry County, Kentucky Groom's mother POB: Perry County, Kentucky
Date of marriage: 29 September 1890
Bride: Oley Campbell Residence: Leslie County, Kentucky Age: 18 Number of Marriages: None Bride's POB: Perry County, Kentucky Bride's father POB: Clay County, Kentucky Bride's mother POB: Perry County, Kentucky
Remarks: Abijah Campbell father of the bride.
Marriage Book 7, page 399

Groom: James Stidham Residence: Leslie County, Kentucky Age: 22 Number of Marriages: Blank Occupation: Farmer Groom's POB: Perry County, Kentucky Groom's father POB: Perry County, Kentucky Groom's mother POB: Perry County, Kentucky
Date of marriage: 2 January 1892
Bride: Nancy Shepherd Residence: Leslie County, Kentucky Age: 21 Number of Marriages: Blank Bride's POB: Perry County, Kentucky Bride's father POB: Blank Bride's mother POB: Blank Marriage Book 7, page 465

Groom: James Stidham Residence: Leslie County, Kentucky Age: 25 Number of Marriages: Farmer Occupation: Farmer Groom's POB: Perry County, Kentucky Groom's father POB: Blank Groom's mother POB: Blank
Date of marriage: 1 September 1894

Bride: Sis Asher Residence: Leslie County, Kentucky Age: 25 Number of Marriages: Blank Bride's POB: Perry County, Kentucky Bride's father POB: Blank Bride's mother POB: Blank Marriage Book 7, page 629

Groom: John Stidham Residence: Leslie County, Kentucky Age: 21 Number of Marriages: Blank Occupation: Farmer Groom's POB: Harlan County, Kentucky Groom's father POB: Harlan County, Kentucky Groom's mother POB: Harlan County, Kentucky
Date of marriage: 2 February 1886
Bride: Elizabeth Shepherd Residence: Leslie County, Kentucky Age: 18 Number of Marriages: Blank Bride's POB: Perry County, Kentucky Bride's father POB: Perry County, Kentucky Bride's mother POB: Perry County, Kentucky Marriage Book 7, page 37

Groom: John Stidham Residence: Leslie County, Kentucky Age: 28 Number of Marriages: 1 Occupation: Farmer Groom's POB: Perry County, Kentucky Groom's father POB: Blank Groom's mother POB: Blank
Date of marriage: 1 April 1893
Bride: Adel Young Residence: Leslie County, Kentucky Age: 29 Number of Marriages: 1 Bride's POB: Perry County, Kentucky Bride's father POB: Harlan County, Kentucky Bride's mother POB: Clay County, Kentucky Marriage Book 7, page 545

Groom: Shiloh Stidham Residence: Leslie County, Kentucky Age: 17 Number of Marriages: Blank Occupation: Farmer Groom's POB: Perry County, Kentucky Groom's father POB: Perry County, Kentucky Groom's mother POB: Perry County, Kentucky
Date of marriage: 22 December 1892
Bride: Alley Fields Residence: Leslie County, Kentucky Age: 17 Number of Marriages: Blank Bride's POB: Perry County, Kentucky Bride's father POB: Perry County, Kentucky Bride's mother POB: Perry County, Kentucky Marriage Book 7, page 529

Tarter

Groom: Henry Tarter Residence: Leslie County, Kentucky Age: 19 Number of Marriages: Blank Occupation: Farmer Groom's POB: Hawkins County, Tennessee Groom's father POB: Kentucky Groom's mother POB: Scott County, Virginia
Date of marriage: 19 January 1889
Bride: Sarah Ausburn Residence: Leslie County, Kentucky Age: 26 Number of Marriages: 1 Bride's POB: Blank Bride's father POB: Blank Bride's mother POB: Blank Marriage Book 7, page 263

Taylor

Groom: Pierce Taylor Residence: Leslie County, Kentucky Age: 23
Number of Marriages: 1 Occupation: Farmer Groom's POB: Knox County, Kentucky Groom's father POB: Blank Groom's mother POB: Blank
Date of marriage: 19 April 1888
Bride: Alice Roberts Residence: Leslie County, Kentucky Age: 34 Number of Marriages: Blank Bride's POB: Blank Bride's father POB: Blank Bride's mother POB: Blank Marriage Book 7, Page 221

Templeton

Groom: Marian Templeton Residence: Leslie County, Kentucky Age: 19
Number of Marriages: Blank Occupation: Farmer Groom's POB: Harlan County, Kentucky Groom's father POB: Harlan County, Kentucky Groom's mother POB: Harlan County, Kentucky
Date of marriage: 10 August 1885
Bride: Rebecca Jane York Residence: Leslie County, Kentucky Age: 20 Number of Marriages: Blank Bride's POB: Harlan County, Kentucky Bride's father POB: Blank Bride's mother POB: Blank Marriage Book 7, Page 15

Thomas

Groom: Daniel Thomas Residence: Leslie County, Kentucky Age: 22
Number of Marriages: Blank Occupation: Farmer Groom's POB: Harlan County, Kentucky Groom's father POB: Harlan County, Kentucky Groom's mother POB: Harlan County, Kentucky
Date of marriage: 7 October 1893
Bride: Susan Vanover Residence: Leslie County, Kentucky Age: 18 Number of Marriages: Blank Bride's POB: Perry County, Kentucky Bride's father POB: Blank Bride's mother POB: Blank
Remarks: The following note appears in the record: "October 7, 1893. To the Clerk of Leslie County Court. You are authorized to give license to Dan Thomas and Susan Vanover. Signed A. L. Vanover."
Marriage Book 7, page 569

Thompson

Groom: Joseph Thompson Residence: Leslie County, Kentucky Age: 18
Number of Marriages: Blank Occupation: Farmer Groom's POB: Perry County, Kentucky Groom's father POB: Virginia Groom's mother POB: Kentucky
Date of marriage: 23 February 1887

Bride: Matilda Joseph Residence: Leslie County, Kentucky Age: 18
Number of Marriages: Blank Bride's POB: Perry County, Kentucky Bride's father POB: Blank Bride's mother POB: Blank Marriage Book 7, page 123

Turner

Groom: David Y. Turner Residence: Leslie County, Kentucky Age: 24
Number of Marriages: 1 Occupation: Farmer Groom's POB: Harlan County, Kentucky Groom's father POB: Harlan County, Kentucky Groom's mother POB: Harlan County, Kentucky
Date of marriage: 7 October 1893
Bride: Susan E. Baker Residence: Leslie County, Kentucky Age: 18
Number of Marriages: Blank Bride's POB: Perry County, Kentucky Bride's father POB: Blank Bride's mother POB: Blank Marriage Book 7, page 571

Valance

Groom: Alexander Valance Residence: Kentucky Age: 35 Number of Marriages: Blank Occupation: Mining coal Groom's POB: Blank Groom's father POB: Blank Groom's mother POB: Blank
Date of marriage: 25 May 1891
Bride: Jane Roberts Residence: Clay County, Kentucky Age: 30 Number of Marriages: 1 Bride's POB: Clay County, Kentucky Bride's father POB: Clay County, Kentucky Bride's mother POB: Clay County, Kentucky
Marriage Book 7, page 427

Valentine

Groom: Madison Valentine Residence: Perry County, Kentucky Age: 20
Number of Marriages: Blank Occupation: Farmer Groom's POB: Perry County, Kentucky Groom's father POB: Perry County, Kentucky Groom's mother POB: Perry County, Kentucky
Date of marriage: 21 December 1888
Bride: Perline Baker Residence: Perry County, Kentucky Age: 16 Number of Marriages: Blank Bride's POB: Jackson County, Kentucky Bride's father POB: Blank Bride's mother POB: Blank
Remarks: Not in the record reads as follows: "August 8th, 1889. This is to certify that the County Court Clerk is authorized to issue license of matrimony to our daughter, Rachel Melton. Given under our hand and date above written. Signed Preston Melton. Signed: Sally Melton. // December 20th,'88. Clerk of Leslie County. Please to issue license for Perline Baker and Madison Valentine. Signed: Robert Baker. // December 20, '88. Clerk of Leslie County. Please to issue for Madison Valentine and Perline Baker. Signed: Wade Valentine."

Marriage Book 7, page 257

Vanover

Groom: Andrew Vanover Residence: Leslie County, Kentucky Age: 22 Number of Marriages: Blank Occupation: Farmer Groom's POB: Letcher County, Kentucky Groom's father POB: North Carolina Groom's mother POB: North Carolina
Date of marriage: 2 September 1890
Bride: Nancy Margate Eversole Residence: Perry County, Kentucky Age: 17 Number of Marriages: Blank Bride's POB: Perry County, Kentucky Bride's father POB: Perry County, Kentucky Bride's mother POB: Perry County, Kentucky
Remarks: The following note appears in the record: "Mr. Matson Howard. Give Andrew Vanover license to marry my Nancy Margate. Signed: Thomas Eversole."
Marriage Book 7, page 385

Wells

Groom: Arch Wells Residence: Blank Age: Blank Number of Marriages: Blank Occupation: Blank Groom's POB: Blank Groom's father POB: Blank Groom's mother POB: Blank
Date of marriage: 29 November 1894
Bride: Sallie Stidham Residence: Blank Age: Blank Number of Marriages: Blank Bride's POB: Blank Bride's father POB: Blank Bride's mother POB: Blank
Remarks: Only page for marriage bond exists.
Marriage Book 7, page 640

West

Groom: James West Residence: Leslie County, Kentucky Age: 19 Number of Marriages: Blank Occupation: Farmer Groom's POB: Clay County, Kentucky Groom's father POB: Perry County, Kentucky Groom's mother POB: Clay County, Kentucky
Date of marriage: 27 August 1886
Bride: Jane Williams Residence: Leslie County, Kentucky Age: About 27 Number of Marriages: 1 Bride's POB: Perry County, Kentucky Bride's father POB: Perry County, Kentucky Bride's mother POB: Perry County, Kentucky
Remarks: Note in the record reads as follows: "Mr. J. M. Howard. You will send me my license. I have not got the change now but I will pay you in a short time and oblige yours. Signed: W. J. Collett /// Mr. J. M. Howard. You

are directed to give Nancy Collett marriage license to Manny. Signed: W. J. Collett this September 25 1886 signed: His mark "X" Samuel Collett."
Marriage Book 7, page 99

Groom: William West Residence: Perry County, Kentucky Age: 18 Number of Marriages: 1 Occupation: Farmer Groom's POB: Perry County, Kentucky Groom's father POB: Perry County, Kentucky Groom's mother POB: Perry County, Kentucky
Date of marriage: 29 November 1888
Bride: Sally Estep Residence: Perry County, Kentucky Age: 18 Number of Marriages: 1 Bride's POB: Perry County, Kentucky Bride's father POB: Perry County, Kentucky Bride's mother POB: Perry County, Kentucky
Remarks: Note appears in the record as follows: I do agree for William West to obtain license to marry my girl. Signed: His mark "X" Samson Estep. // November 26, 1888. William Rice and Rebecca Rice here by authorized the Clerk of Leslie County, Kentucky to give marriage license for Henry Rice and Sally Estep."
Marriage Book 7, page 253

Whitehead

Groom: Taylor Whitehead Residence: Leslie County, Kentucky Age: 21 Number of Marriages: Blank Occupation: Farmer Groom's POB: Clay County, Kentucky Groom's father POB: Blank Groom's mother POB: Blank
Date of marriage: 21 December 1887
Bride: Becca Jane Baker Residence: Leslie County, Kentucky Age: 17 Number of Marriages: Blank Bride's POB: Perry County, Kentucky Bride's father POB: Perry County, Kentucky Bride's mother POB: Perry County, Kentucky Marriage Book 7, Page 183

Wilder

Groom: Alfred Wilder Residence: Leslie County, Kentucky Age: 21 Number of Marriages: Blank Occupation: Farmer Groom's POB: Clay County, Kentucky Groom's father POB: Clay County, Kentucky Groom's mother POB: Clay County, Kentucky
Date of marriage: 19 May 1892
Bride: Mary Sisemore Residence: Leslie County, Kentucky Age: 21 Number of Marriages: Blank Bride's POB: Perry County, Kentucky Bride's father POB: Clay County, Kentucky Bride's mother POB: Clay County, Kentucky Marriage Book 7, page 489

Groom: Henry Wilder Residence: Clay County, Kentucky Age: 20 Number of Marriages: Blank Occupation: Farmer Groom's POB: Clay County, Kentucky Groom's father POB: Clay County, Kentucky Groom's mother POB: Clay County, Kentucky
Date of marriage: 24 September 1894
Bride: May Collins Residence: Leslie County, Kentucky Age: 19 Number of Marriages: Blank Bride's POB: Clay County, Kentucky Bride's father POB: Clay County, Kentucky Bride's mother POB: Clay County, Kentucky
Marriage Book 7, page 633

Williams

Groom: J. B. Williams Residence: Leslie County, Kentucky Age: 30 Number of Marriages: 1 Occupation: Farmer Groom's POB: Perry County, Kentucky Groom's father POB: Perry County, Kentucky Groom's mother POB: Perry County, Kentucky
Date of marriage: 15 February 1886
Bride: Cassey Wills Residence: Leslie County, Kentucky Age: 19 Number of Marriages: Blank Bride's POB: Perry County, Kentucky Bride's father POB: Wise County, Virginia Bride's mother POB: Wise County, Virginia
Marriage Book 7, Page 39

Groom: Nathaniel Williams Residence: Leslie County, Kentucky Age: 21 Number of Marriages: Blank Occupation: Farmer Groom's POB: Perry County, Kentucky Groom's father POB: Blank Groom's mother POB: Blank
Date of marriage: 6 April 1886
Bride: Nancy Ingle Residence: Leslie County, Kentucky Age: 22 Number of Marriages: 1 Bride's POB: Perry County, Kentucky Bride's father POB: Blank Bride's mother POB: Blank Marriage Book 7, Page 55

Groom: Nathaniel Williams Residence: Leslie County, Kentucky Age: 21 Number of Marriages: Blank Occupation: Farmer Groom's POB: Perry County, Kentucky Groom's father POB: Virginia Groom's mother POB: Virginia
Date of marriage: 3 November 1886
Bride: Nancy Kilburn Residence: Leslie County, Kentucky Age: 21 Number of Marriages: Blank Bride's POB: Perry County, Kentucky Bride's father POB: Blank Bride's mother POB: Perry County, Kentucky Marriage Book 7, page 111

Groom: Thomas W. Williams Residence: Leslie County, Kentucky Age: 44 Number of Marriages: 1 Occupation: Clerk Groom's POB: Ohio Groom's father POB: Ohio Groom's mother POB: Ohio

Date of marriage: 26 August 1891
Bride: Mary Jane Dixon Residence: Leslie County, Kentucky Age: 32
Number of Marriages: 1 Bride's POB: Perry County, Kentucky Bride's
father POB: Blank Bride's mother POB: Blank Marriage Book 7, page 437

Witt

Groom: Alfred Witt Residence: Leslie County, Kentucky Age: 18 Number
of Marriages: Blank Occupation: Farmer Groom's POB: Perry County,
Kentucky Groom's father POB: Lee County, Kentucky Groom's mother
POB: Perry County, Kentucky
Date of marriage: 26 July 1886
Bride: Elender Gross Residence: Leslie County, Kentucky Age: 31
Number of Marriages: 1 Bride's POB: Letcher County, Kentucky Bride's
father POB: Blank Bride's mother POB: Blank Marriage Book 7, Page 83

Groom: James Witt Residence: Leslie County, Kentucky Age: 19 Number
of Marriages: Blank Occupation: Farmer Groom's POB: Rockcastle County,
Kentucky Groom's father POB: Blank Groom's mother POB: Blank
Date of marriage: 8 November 1890
Bride: Elizabeth Pennington Residence: Leslie County, Kentucky Age: 17
Number of Marriages: Blank Bride's POB: Perry County, Kentucky Bride's
father POB: Blank Bride's mother POB: Blank Marriage Book 7, page 407

Wombles

Groom: Henry Wombles Residence: Leslie County, Kentucky Age: 20
Number of Marriages: Blank Occupation: Farmer Groom's POB: Clay
County, Kentucky Groom's father POB: Clay County, Kentucky Groom's
mother POB: Clay County, Kentucky
Date of marriage: 12 November 1885
Bride: Ellen Sisemore Residence: Leslie County, Kentucky Age: 16
Number of Marriages: Blank Bride's POB: Clay County, Kentucky Bride's
father POB: Clay County, Kentucky Bride's mother: POB: Clay County,
Kentucky Marriage Book 7, page 21

Woods

Groom: Felix Woods Residence: Leslie County, Kentucky Age: 34
Number of Marriages: 1 Occupation: Farmer Groom's POB: Clay County,
Kentucky Groom's father POB: Clay County, Kentucky Groom's mother
POB: Clay County, Kentucky
Date of marriage: 29 December 1887

Bride: Polly Baker Residence: Leslie County, Kentucky Age: 17 Number of Marriages: Blank Bride's POB: Perry County, Kentucky Bride's father POB: Perry County, Kentucky Bride's mother POB: Blank Marriage Book 7, page 189

Groom: Pleasant Woods Residence: Leslie County, Kentucky Age: Blank Number of Marriages: Blank Occupation: Farmer Groom's POB: Blank Groom's father POB: Blank Groom's mother POB: Blank
Date of marriage: 7 July 1886
Bride: Nancy Asher Residence: Leslie County, Kentucky Age: Blank Number of Marriages: Blank Bride's POB: Blank Bride's father POB: Blank Bride's mother POB: Blank
Remarks: Note in the record reads as follows: "This is to certify to county court clerk of Leslie County that Pleasant Woods is authorized to sign a certificate or order marriage license for my daughter. July 8, 1886. Signed: Jerry Woods.
Marriage Book 7, page 77

Wooton

Groom: Finley Wooton Residence: Leslie County, Kentucky Age: 21 Number of Marriages: 1 Occupation: Farmer Groom's POB: Perry County, Kentucky Groom's father POB: Perry County, Kentucky Groom's mother POB: Perry County, Kentucky
Date of marriage: 22 October 1892
Bride: Susan Lewis Residence: Leslie County, Kentucky Age: 16 Number of Marriages: 1 Bride's POB: Perry County, Kentucky Bride's father POB: Perry County, Kentucky Bride's mother POB: Perry County, Kentucky
Marriage Book 7, page 519

Groom: Jackson Wooton Residence: Leslie County, Kentucky Age: 36 Number of Marriages: 1 Occupation: Farmer Groom's POB: Perry County, Kentucky Groom's father POB: Perry County, Kentucky Groom's mother POB: Perry County, Kentucky
Date of marriage: 6 April 1889
Bride: Liza Morgan Residence: Leslie County, Kentucky Age: 16 Number of Marriages: Blank Bride's POB: Clay County, Kentucky Bride's father POB: Clay County, Kentucky Bride's mother POB: Clay County, Kentucky
Marriage Book 7, page 287

Groom: John H. Wooton Residence: Leslie County, Kentucky Age: 28 Number of Marriages: 1 Occupation: Farmer Groom's POB: Perry County, Kentucky Groom's father POB: Perry County, Kentucky Groom's mother POB: Perry County, Kentucky

Date of marriage: 26 November 1885
Bride: Polly Ann Shepherd Residence: Leslie County, Kentucky Age: 20
Number of Marriages: 1 Bride's POB: Perry County, Kentucky Bride's father POB: Perry County, Kentucky Bride's mother POB: Perry County, Kentucky Marriage Book 7, page 25

Groom: John M. Wooton Residence: Leslie County, Kentucky Age: 18
Number of Marriages: Blank Occupation: Farmer Groom's POB: Perry County, Kentucky Groom's father POB: Perry County, Kentucky Groom's mother POB: Perry County, Kentucky
Date of marriage: 23 March 1889
Bride: Polly Margaret Feltner Residence: Leslie County, Kentucky Age: 16
Number of Marriages: Blank Bride's POB: Perry County, Kentucky Bride's father POB: Perry County, Kentucky Bride's mother POB: Perry County, Kentucky
Remarks: Note appears in the record as follows: "Mr. J. M. Howard, Clerk of Leslie County Court. Please issue license for my daughter, Polly Margaret Feltner and John Wooton to marry. This 23rd of March 1889. Signed: Russel Feltner."
Marriage Book 7, page 283

Groom: Russel Wooton Residence: Leslie County, Kentucky Age: 27
Number of Marriages: 1 Occupation: Farmer Groom's POB: Perry County, Kentucky Groom's father POB: Perry County, Kentucky Groom's mother POB: Perry County, Kentucky
Date of marriage: 14 February 1889
Bride: Elizabeth Asher Residence: Leslie County, Kentucky Age: 27
Number of Marriages: Blank Bride's POB: Perry County, Kentucky Bride's father POB: Blank Bride's mother POB: Blank Marriage Book 7, page 269

Groom: Russel Wooton Residence: Leslie County, Kentucky Age: 28
Number of Marriages: 3 Occupation: Farmer Groom's POB: Perry County, Kentucky Groom's father POB: Perry County, Kentucky Groom's mother POB: Perry County, Kentucky
Date of marriage: 24 March 1890
Bride: Polly Jane Asher Residence: Leslie County, Kentucky Age: 21
Number of Marriages: Blank Bride's POB: Perry County, Kentucky Bride's father POB: Blank Bride's mother POB: Blank Marriage Book 7, page 357

Groom: William D. Wooton Residence: Leslie County, Kentucky Age: 38
Number of Marriages: 2 Occupation: Farmer Groom's POB: Perry County, Kentucky Groom's father POB: Perry County, Kentucky Groom's mother POB: Perry County, Kentucky
Date of marriage: 30 April 1887

Bride: Nancy Maggard Residence: Leslie County, Kentucky Age: 20 Number of Marriages: 1 Bride's POB: Perry County, Kentucky Bride's father POB: Letcher County, Kentucky Bride's mother POB: Scott County, Virginia Marriage Book 7, page 143

Groom: Wilson Wooton Residence: Hyden, Leslie County, Kentucky Age: 25 Number of Marriages: Blank Occupation: Lawyer Groom's POB: Perry County, Kentucky Groom's father POB: Blank Groom's mother POB: Perry County, Kentucky
Date of marriage: 2 July 1887
Bride: Martha Ann Roberts Residence: Leslie County, Kentucky Age: 21 Number of Marriages: 2 Bride's POB: Perry County, Kentucky Bride's father POB: Perry County, Kentucky Bride's mother POB: Perry County, Kentucky Marriage Book 7, page 153

Yates

Groom: Howard Yates Residence: Leslie County, Kentucky Age: 18 Number of Marriages: Blank Occupation: Farmer Groom's POB: Harlan County, Kentucky Groom's father POB: Blank Groom's mother POB: Blank
Date of marriage: January 1877
Bride: Susan Causey Residence: Leslie County, Kentucky Age: 16 Number of Marriages: Blank Bride's POB: Perry County, Kentucky Bride's father POB: Blank Bride's mother POB: Blank Marriage Book 7, Page 121

Young

Groom: Emanuel Young Residence: Leslie County, Kentucky Age: 23 Number of Marriages: Blank Occupation: Farmer Groom's POB: Perry County, Kentucky Groom's father POB: Kentucky Groom's mother POB: Kentucky
Date of marriage: 19 January 1892
Bride: Sarah Shepherd Residence: Leslie County, Kentucky Age: 25 Number of Marriages: 1 Bride's POB: Perry County, Kentucky Bride's father POB: Blank Bride's mother POB: Blank Marriage Book 7, page 471

Groom: Samuel Young Residence: Hyden, Kentucky Age: 28 Number of Marriages: 3 Occupation: Mechanic Groom's POB: Perry County, Kentucky Groom's father POB: North Carolina Groom's mother POB: North Carolina
Date of marriage: 31 October 1887
Bride: Nancy Muncy Residence: Hyden, Kentucky Age: 21 Number of Marriages: 1 Bride's POB: Clay County, Kentucky Bride's father POB:

Clay County, Kentucky Bride's mother POB: Clay County, Kentucky Marriage Book 7, page 173

Index

Abshier
  A. J., 3
Adams
  John, 3
Anderson
  Christopher, 3, 42
  M. L., 42
Asburn
  Rachel, 45
Asher
  Andrew, 4
  Elizabeth, 42, 90
  Emily, 26, 39
  John, 4
  Judia, 45
  Lucindia, 79
  Martha, 65
  Mary, 43
  Nancy, 89
  Polly Ann, 45
  Polly Jane, 91
  Randall, 4
  Sis, 81
  Susan, 43
  Timothy, 5
Ausburn
  Levi, 5
  Sarah, 82
Bailey
  Elizabeth, 72
  Hannah, 12
  J. M., 6
  Minter, 6
Baker
  Adam, 6
  Becca Jane, 86
  Betty Ann, 75
  Cathy, 3
  El Jane, 7
  Eliza, 17
  Henry, 3

  Judia, 32, 38
  L. G., 59, 75
  Louisa, 6
  Lucy Ann, 9
  Martha, 3, 19
  Parilee, 8
  Perline, 84
  Polly, 42, 89
  Russel, 6
  Sallie, 44
  Samuel, 6
  Susan E., 59, 84
  William, 7, 17, 44
Banks
  Susannah, 33
Barger
  Andrew, 34
  Delaney, 7, 72
  Martha, 34
  Merica, 13
Begley
  Abner, 7
  Dosa, 61
  Elijah, 7
  Elizabeth, 9
  F. G., 8
  Felix G., 8
  Garret, 8
  Granville, 8
  John Y., 9
  Lafayette, 9
  Lilly, 50
  Martha, 50
  Mary, 58
  Robert, 9
  Sally, 78
  Susan, 26, 28
Bentley
  W. P., 9
Bishop
  Jane, 34

Blevins
  Francis, 12
Boggs
  Charlotte, 55
  Elizabeth, 19
  J. C., 8
  Margaret, 8
  Nancy J., 28
  Timothy, 10
Bolin
  Pallis, 10
Bollin
  Polly, 39
Bond
  Preston, 10
Bowling
  Elizabeth, 73
  Jesse B., 73
  Jon E., 62
  Nancy, 62
  Sally, 62
  William, 10
Brock
  Nancy, 11
  Washington, 11
Brown
  Ella, 17
  J. C., 11
Browning
  Don Juan, 11
  Hannah, 44
  Jan, 7
  Sarah J., 41
  Stephen, 41
  Victory, 14
Buckhead
  Silvania, 26
Burkhart
  S. C., 67
  Silvania, 67
Burns
  Abijah, 11, 12
Caldwell
  J. M., 12

Calihan
  Lucinda, 80
  Lucindy, 80
Campbell
  Abijah, 12, 81
  Oley, 81
  William, 12
Causey
  C. B., 23
  Lucinda, 23
  Susan, 91
Clark
  James, 5
  Luvina, 53
Clarkston
  Merica, 10
Collett
  Jackson, 13
  James, 13
  Nancy, 13, 85
  Samuel, 86
  W. J., 13, 85, 86
Collins
  George, 13
  Henry, 14
  Jan, 24
  John, 14
  Lucinda, 15
  Lucindy, 75
  May, 87
  Robert, 4, 14, 75
  Sally Ann, 67
  Tabitha Ellen, 4, 15
  Thomas, 14
  Ulysses G., 4, 14
  Vinie, 72
  Washington, 15
  William, 15, 16, 75
Colwell
  Nesbia, 16
Combs
  Andrew, 16
  Elizabeth, 77
  Jackson, 16, 17

Orleana, 58
Preston, 17
Sarah, 17
Coots
  Ance, 17
  James, 18
  James H., 18
  Maryan, 18
  Sarah, 10
  Sylvester, 18
  William, 18
  William D., 18
Cope
  Arrend, 35
  Arrend C., 35
  Emmanuel, 35
  Julia A., 47
Cornett
  Elizabeth Jane, 25
  Fred, 19
  Granville, 19
  Rachel Jane, 28
  Rebecca, 68
  Robert, 19
  William, 18, 19, 28
Couch
  A. B., 20
  Anderson, 20
  Cole, 65
  Elizabeth, 38
  Felix, 20
  Harrison, 20, 21
  Jesse, 57
  John, 21, 22
  Martha, 14, 65
  Orlenia, 38
  Peggie, 48
  Sally, 20
  Sarah, 64
  Wilk, 21
  Wilkerson, 21
  William, 21, 22
Creech
  J. M., 22

  James, 22
Cress
  John, 22
  Levi, 23
  William, 23
Daniel
  Martha J., 48, 49
Daniels
  C. B., 23
Davidson
  Belle Gerry, 24
  Frank, 24
  Hiram, 24
  Loyd, 24
  Sally Ann, 20
Davis
  Hiram B., 24, 25
Day
  Henry, 25
  Nancy, 37
  W. H., 25
Dixon
  A. B., 58
  John L., 25
  Leander, 26
  Mary Jane, 88
  William, 26
Duff
  Andrew Jackson, 26
  Jackson, 67
Eastridge
  F. G., 26, 27
  Polly, 69
Eldridge
  William, 27
Estep
  Sally, 70, 86
  Samson, 86
Eversole
  Abner, 27
  Alexander, 27
  Elizabeth, 24
  J. M., 28
  Lucy, 53

Nancy Margate, 85
  Thomas, 85
  W. B., 28
Farler
  French, 28
  Sarah, 56
Farmer
  Arpha, 48
  H. J., 48
  John C., 29
  W. A., 29
Fee
  James L., 29
  Mary Jane, 14
Feltner
  E. B., 29
  Ellen, 30
  Esaw, 30
  Felix, 30
  Harrison, 30
  Jackson, 31, 54
  John, 31
  Lucindia, 51
  M. B., 31, 62
  Madison, 32
  N. B., 32
  Polly Margaret, 90
  Rachel Jane, 4
  Rebecca, 40
  Russel, 54, 90
  Sarah Bell, 31, 54
Fields
  Alley, 82
  Emanuel, 32
  Sallie, 52
  Sally Ann, 52
  William H., 33
Flanery
  W. H., 63
  William H., 33
Ford
  Katie, 41
France
  Hansford, 50

  Nancy, 50
Freeman
  Louisa, 5
French
  Mallie, 6
Gay
  Elijah, 33
  John, 33
  Nelson, 34
  Polly, 71
  William, 34
Gibson
  Constance, 80
  James, 34
  Lucindia, 79
  Martha, 71
  Sim, 80
Gilbert
  Miller, 35
Griffitt
  Jacob, 35
  James, 35
Griffitts
  Elizabeth, 71
  Nancy Ann, 36
Gross
  Elender, 88
  J. B., 35
Gross, Jr.
  J. B., Jr., 35
Gross, Sr.
  J. B., Sr., 35
Hacker
  John, 36
  Sylvania, 52
Hamilton
  Olley, 18
Hampton
  Mary, 10
Hart
  Dora Jane, 53
Hast
  E. L., 36
Hayes

Hiram H., 36
Hazelwood
  G. M., 36
Helton
  Carter, 16
  Ellen, 16
  Martha, 58
Hensley
  America, 34
  Nancy, 15
  Nancy Jane, 14
  Susan, 33
Henson
  William, 37
Herd
  Jacob, 37
Hibbard
  Jackson, 37
Hignight
  Elihu, 38
  Elizabeth, 7
  Ellen, 9
Holland
  James C., 38
Hollen
  Thomas, 38
Hooker
  Catherine, 35
Hoskins
  Annie, 37
  Armilda, 12
  E. L., 38
  Felix, 39
  H. C., 39
  Irvine, 27
  Isaac, 39
  John, 39
  Polly, 32
  Russel, 40
  Serena, 26, 27
  William R., 40
Howard
  Alice, 66
  Andrew, 40

  Betty, 34
  Dan, 76
  David D., 41
  E. C. G., 75
  Ella J., 60
  Felix, 41
  Gilbert, 67
  H. J., 41
  Henry J., 41
  Isaac, 42
  J. M., 6, 8, 12, 17, 18, 21, 23,
    24, 27, 30, 31, 35, 39, 41,
    42, 45, 50, 52, 54, 59, 60,
    63, 65, 68, 74, 75, 76, 77,
    78, 85, 90
  Jackson, 21, 78
  James, 41
  Jesse, 42
  John, 43
  John L., 42
  Julyan, 11
  Lee, 43
  M., 15
  Madison, 23, 42, 74
  Martha, 78
  Mary Jane, 29, 78
  Mat, 22, 25, 35, 66
  Matson, 85
  Mattison, 70
  Mr., 49
  Peggy, 59
  Polly, 21, 69
  Rodslia, 19
  Zachariah, 43
Hubbard
  E., 29
Huff
  Simpson, 43
Ingle
  Annie, 17
  Jane, 25
  John, 44
  Nancy, 87
  Sarah, 25

William, 44
Irvin
  Ezekiel, 44
Johnson
  Elizabeth, 70
  Joseph, 45
  Polly, 64
  Thomas, 64
Jones
  Cordelia, 5
  Cordillie, 73
  Edmon, 45
  Harvey, 45
  Hughes, 45
  Irvin, 46
  Mary Elizabeth, 46
  Vina, 37
  William, 46
Joseph
  Jan, 35
  Jane, 35
  Matilda, 83
  Reason, 46
Kennedy
  John, 46
Kilbourn
  Cassie, 53
Kilburn
  John, 47
  Nancy, 87
Langdon
  Alfred, 47
  Olena, 36
  Sam Alfred, 43
  Simeon, 43
Ledford
  Granville, 5
  Susannah, 5
Lewis
  A. C., 47, 48
  Abner, 48
  Daniel, 48
  David, 18, 63
  David Y., 27
  E. D., 24
  E. L., 48
  Elizabeth, 21, 50, 62, 63
  Ellen, 22
  Emily, 4
  Fannie, 49
  H. D., 49
  Harrison, 49
  Henry D., 49
  Ira, 49
  J. H., 49
  James, 50, 63, 78
  James L., 50
  Jeff, 23
  Jesevine, 19
  Jesse, 76
  John, 30, 49, 50
  John C., 22
  Juder, 21
  Judia, 80
  Levi, 27
  Lucinda, 20
  Malinda, 76
  Margaret, 3, 30
  Margie, 30
  R. J., 51
  Rutha J., 40
  S. J., 51
  Samuel, 51
  Sarah, 48
  Susan, 89
  William, 51, 52
Maggard
  A. B., 53
  A. J., 53
  Anna, 72
  Israel, 53
  John A., 54
  Lucy J., 22
  Nancy, 91
  Reuben, 53
  Rutha Jane, 57
  W. J., 54
  W. R., 53

William, 54
Mattingly
  M. J., 58
  Mary, 58
  Mary Sally, 58
McCollum
  Willis, 54, 68
McDaniel
  Daniel, 55
  Lucy, 75
McKenney
  Richard, 55
McKinney
  Daniel, 55
  William, 55
Melton
  Abner F., 56
  Elizabeth, 57
  Nancy, 9
  Preston, 84
  Rachel, 57, 84
  Rhoda, 55
  Russel, 56
  Sally, 84
  William, 56
Messer
  Benjamin, 56
  Madison, 57
  Susan, 56
Metcalf
  Prelia, 59
Miller
  George W., 57
Miniard
  Joseph, 17, 57
Morgan
  A. B., 52, 57, 58, 72
  Alice, 52
  Fannie, 51
  G. M., 58
  G. W., 29, 58, 77
  Garland, 58
  Hughes, 59
  Ira, 59

  James, 59
  Jane, 59
  John E., 59
  Liza, 90
  Lucy, 39
  Martha, 51
  Nancy, 29, 67
  Sarah J., 29
  Taylor, 60
  Thomas, 60
Morris
  G. O., 60
  Rebecca, 65
Mosley
  Henderson, 60
  Samuel, 42
  Sarah, 42
Mullins
  W. J., 61
Muncy
  Allen, 61
  Jasper, 61
  John, 62
  Mary, 69
  Nancy, 92
Murrell
  Grant, 62
Nance
  Hannah, 66
  William, 62
Nantz
  Dan, 63
  Daniel, 63
  John, 63
  Martha, 78
Napier
  A. B., 63
  Adrian, 64
  Alice, 60
  Arra, 78
  Ballard, 64
  Catherine, 30
  Dillion, 64
  E. Z., 22

Elizabeth, 11, 27
Emeriah, 24
H. N., 31, 62
Hamp, 68
Henry, 64
J. N., 78
Jack, 65
Jackson, 65
Jane, 31
John, 65
John Hampton, 64
Kinyard, 63
Kissie, 47
Lincoln, 65
Lucindy, 79
M. E., 26
Martha, 76
Mc, 66
Molly, 60
Nancy, 23
Polly Jane, 22
Rachel Jane, 23
Rebecca, 32, 54, 62, 63
Rebecca Jane, 39
Sara, 20
Sarah, 21
Susan, 43, 61
Vina, 23
William, 66
Noe
  Sarah, 69
North
  Nannie, 30
  Wilson, 66
Oliver
  James, 66
  Sherman, 67
Osbourne
  William, 12
Pace
  Nancy, 71, 72
  Sarah, 55
  William, 67
Parker

Elijah, 67
Franklin, 67
Nancy, 67
Parks
  Hiram, 68
  William, 68
Pennington
  Alex, 68
  Elizabeth, 44, 45, 88
  James, 68
  Jesse, 45
  Johnathan, 69
  Lucindia, 49
  Mary E., 45
  Phoebe, 7
  Rosannah, 46
  Sarah, 27
  William, 69
Peters
  Elijah, 79
Press
  Ellicott, 23
Rice
  Frank, 70
  Henry, 70, 86
  Rebecca, 86
  William, 86
Roark
  Hance, 70
  Henderson, 70
  Manervy, 27
Roberts
  Abijah, 70
  Alice, 82
  Anderson, 71
  Bijha, 61
  Fannie, 24
  Felix, 71
  Frank, 71
  James, 72
  James A., 71
  Jane, 76, 84
  Lizzie, 49
  M. C., 72

Martha, 4, 49
Martha Ann, 91
Otta, 61
Price, 72
Susan, 71
W. L., 24
Runals
  Marinda, 72
Sandlin
  Carlo, 73
  Estill, 73
  Polly, 25
Saylor
  Mahala, 80
Scalf
  David, 73
  Dillion, 73, 74
  James, 74
  Jesse, 74
Sergeant
  Elizabeth, 68
Shepherd
  Clemon, 79
  Elihu, 74
  Elisha, 63
  Eliza Jane, 74
  Elizabeth, 81
  Judia, 33
  Judy, 63
  July Ann, 79
  Mahala, 5
  Nancy, 81
  Polly Ann, 90
  Sarah, 92
  Siseme, 13
  Tilda, 13
  William, 74
Simpson
  Gabreal, 75
Sisemore
  Arra, 42
  Array, 43
  Blevins, 43
  Ellen, 13, 64, 88

  Emiline, 75
  Emily, 77
  Henry, 75
  Hiram, 75, 76
  India, 74
  Ira, 76
  James, 76, 77
  Jane, 64
  Joanah, 77
  Joseph, 77
  Killy, 73
  Louisa, 36
  Lucy, 30
  Mahaly, 70
  Martha, 15
  Mary, 46, 86
  May, 65
  Melda, 62
  Nancy, 30
  Robert, 70, 77
  Sabra, 70
  Sallie, 57
  Semmie, 66
  William, 77, 78
Sizemore
  Adaline, 73
  Blevins, 43
  Chaney, 8
  Henry, 75
  James, 76
  John, 15
  Lucy, 63
  Luther, 78
  William, 78
Skeens
  Leander, 79
Smith
  J. Sara, 79
  Sarah, 8
  William, 79
South
  Mary Jane, 10
Sparks
  Artha, 80

Spurlock
  David, 79, 80
  Jess, 80
  John, 80
Stamper
  Lethie Ann, 25
Status
  Rilda, 32
Stewart
  William, 80
Stidham
  Henderson, 80
  Jackson, 81
  James, 81
  Jane, 40, 60
  John, 81
  Maryan, 41
  Nancy Jane, 33
  Rebecca, 68
  Sallie, 85
  Sally, 24
  Sarah, 51
  Shiloh, 82
  Sinda, 55
  William, 40
Tarter
  Henry, 82
Taylor
  Pierce, 82
Templeton
  Marian, 83
Thomas
  Dan, 83
  Daniel, 83
  Jane, 49
Thompson
  Joseph, 83
Turner
  David, 59
  David Y., 83
Valance
  Alexander, 84
Valentine
  Madison, 84

  Rebecca Ellen, 37
  Wade, 84
Vanover
  A. J., 74
  A. L., 83
  Andrew, 85
  Dora, 74
  E. J., 54
  Nancy, 56
  Patsy, 56
  Susan, 83
Wells
  Arch, 85
  Berry Ann, 68
  Betty Ann, 68
West
  James, 85
  William, 86
Whitehead
  Elizabeth, 61
  Taylor, 86
Wilder
  Alfred, 86
  Henry, 87
Williams
  J. B., 87
  Jane, 85
  Juda, 47
  Judia, 47
  Margaret, 18
  Nathaniel, 47, 87
  Polly, 17, 20
  Thomas W., 88
  William, 18
Wills
  Cassey, 87
Wilson
  Gelanie, 66
  Mary Jane, 18
  Rebecca, 48
Witt
  Alfred, 88
  James, 88
Wombles

Henry, 88
Woods
  Charity, 77
  Felix, 89
  Jerry, 89
  John, 24
  Pleasant, 89
Wooton
  Alice, 54
  Alice E., 54
  Alpha Elizabeth, 43
  Eliza, 46
  Finley, 89
  Jackson, 54, 89
  John, 90
  John H., 90
  John M., 90
  Lisany, 40
  Manda Jane, 3
  Mary Jane, 16
  Nannie, 6
  Polly, 16, 61
  Russel, 90
  Sally, 31
  W. D., 40
  William D., 91
  Wilson, 91
Yates
  Howard, 91
York
  Rebecca Jane, 83
Young
  Adel, 82
  Emanuel, 92
  Samuel, 92

www.ingramcontent.com/pod-product-compliance
Lightning Source LLC
Chambersburg PA
CBHW071743090426
42738CB00011B/2543